TASTES across the STATES

Published by Pediment Publishing, a division of The Pediment Group, Inc.
www.pediment.com • Printed in the United States of America.

Foreword

Welcome to Tastes Across the States — a special compilation of recipes contributed by readers of some of America's leading newspapers.

In October 2020, we asked readers to submit their favorite original family recipes, and we selected a winner from each of the 28 participating national newspapers. Three grand prize winners were then selected in the categories of main dishes, sides and desserts. Our panel of judges combed through more than 600 unique entries, including many with photos taken by proud home chefs.

With such a wealth of finely curated recipes submitted, it became clear that a wider collection of culinary contributions was necessary. The result was Tastes Across the States. We are excited to present the final collection of more than 200 recipes as selected by our team of experts.

Some offer a new twist on old family favorites, while others feature a unique collection of ingredients and preparation that will both challenge and delight. But all come from the kitchens of our loyal readers and reflect the true bounty and diversity of America.

Table of Contents

Main Dishes

Grilled Pork Tenderloin with Pears, Onions and Balsamic Vinegar Glaze

Grilled Pork Tenderloin

- 1 1/2 lbs pork tenderloin
- 1 1/2 Tbsp olive oil
- 1 tsp salt
- 1/4 tsp black pepper
- 1/2 tsp dried minced onion
- 2 cloves garlic, minced
- 1 Tbsp fresh rosemary, minced

Balsamic Vinegar Glaze

- 2 cups balsamic vinegar
- 1/2 cup brown sugar

Pears and Onions

- 1 Tbsp butter
- 1 Tbsp olive oil
- 2 medium Vidalia onions, peeled and each cut into 8 wedges
- 2 large pears, cored and each cut into 8 wedges
- 1/4 cup honey
- 1/2 tsp salt

Total time: 1 hour, 15 minutes
Serves 6

Rinse pork tenderloin; dry well with paper towels. Trim and remove silver skin. Drizzle with olive oil. Combine salt, black pepper, minced onion, garlic and rosemary, and rub all over pork. Allow to rest at room temperature for 20 minutes.

Preheat grill to medium-high heat.

Mix balsamic vinegar and brown sugar in a saucepan over medium heat. Stir constantly until sugar has dissolved. Bring to a boil. Reduce heat to low, and simmer until glaze is reduced by half. Let cool. When cool, it should be the consistency of syrup.

Melt butter with olive oil in a large skillet over medium-high heat. Add the onions and pears. Reduce heat to low, and cook until tender. Stir in honey and salt.

Vinegar reduction, pears and onions can be prepared several hours before grilling.

Sear tenderloin on both sides on grill, then cook until internal temperature is 145 F. (Do not overcook; inside may be slightly pink.) Remove to a serving plate, cover with aluminum foil and let rest for 10 minutes. Uncover, slice into 1/2-inch pieces, top with the pears and onions and drizzle with the balsamic vinegar glaze.

Submitted by: Susan Marbell, National Winner — The News & Observer (Raleigh)

Favorite thing about this recipe: A delicious combination of flavors. Nice to prepare in the fall when local pears are abundant.

Shrimp Napoleon

photo on page 91

Total time: 2 hours
Serves 12

Eggplant

- 2 eggplants, peeled and sliced into 1/4-inch rounds
- 2 cups all-purpose flour
- 1 cup Italian-style breadcrumbs
- 1 1/2 cup Zatarain's Seasoned Fish Fri
- 1/2 cup Tony Chachere's Creole Seasoning
- 4 eggs
- 1/4 cup whole milk
- 2 Tbsp salt
- 16 oz canola oil, for frying

Shrimp and Sauce

- 1/2 onion, chopped
- 2 Tbsp butter
- 1 Tbsp minced garlic
- 2 lbs large shrimp, peeled
- 1/2 tsp Zatarain's Concentrated Liquid Shrimp Boil
- 1 Tbsp Tony Chachere's Creole Seasoning
- 22-oz jar of Prego Roasted Garlic Parmesan Alfredo Sauce
- 22-oz jar of Prego Artisan Four Cheese Alfredo Sauce
- 1 1/2 oz sun-dried tomatoes, chopped
- 1/4 cup fresh Parmesan cheese, grated
- 4 green onions, for garnish

Pasta

- 16 oz angel hair pasta

Peel and slice eggplant into 1/4-inch rounds. Place in salted water; use another bowl to hold eggplant down in water and refrigerate for 30 minutes. Drain and pat dry.

Place flour in a bowl, and in a separate bowl mix breadcrumbs, Fish Fri mix and Tony's seasoning.

In another bowl mix eggs and milk. Dredge eggplant in flour, dip in egg wash, then breadcrumb mixture. Place on single layer and store in fridge for 30 to 60 minutes.

Heat oil to 350 F and fry eggplant in skillet until golden brown.

In a skillet, cook onion in butter until clear. Add garlic, cook until fragrant. Add shrimp, with Tony's and Shrimp Boil. Saute until shrimp is pink and remove from heat.

In a 4-quart saucepan, add sauce, sun-dried tomatoes and Parmesan cheese. Cook on medium until bubbly.

In another 4-quart saucepan, bring water to a boil and add angel hair pasta, cook until al dente.

To plate, place pasta on plate then add 1 or 2 eggplant slices, top with cooked shrimp, pour both jars of sauce over top and garnish with chopped green onions.

Submitted by: Cinda Terrebonne, Local Winner — Sun Herald

Favorite thing about this recipe: It tastes like a culinary chef made it.

Paella

- 4 boneless, skinless chicken thighs
- 4 Italian sausages
- 2 Tbsp vegetable oil
- 2 Tbsp olive oil
- 3/4 cup onion, chopped
- 1 Tbsp garlic, minced
- 3/4 cup carrots, diced
- 3/4 cup yellow and red sweet pepper, chopped
- 1 cup tomatoes, seeded and chopped
- 1/2 cup olives with pimento, diced
- 1 tsp fresh oregano, chopped
- 1/4 tsp saffron
- 1/4 cup capers
- 1/2 cup cilantro, chopped
- 1 tsp red pepper flakes
- 2 1/2 cups water or chicken broth
- 2 1/2 cups dry white wine or beer
- 2 cups paella rice
- 1 lb shrimp, peeled and deveined
- 1 dozen New Zealand clams

Total time: 45 minutes
Serves 6-8

Heat oven to 350 F.

In a paella pan or shallow saute pan with lid, saute chicken and sausage in vegetable oil until just done. Remove from pan and cut into bite-size pieces.

In the same pan, drain oil, use paper towel to absorb any excess. Add olive oil and saute vegetables until slightly tender. Add pimento, oregano, saffron, capers, cilantro and red pepper flakes.

Add broth or water and wine or beer and bring to a slight boil. Add rice and stir together and place in preheated oven for 20 minutes.

Stir in shrimp and place back into the oven for another 10 minutes. Take from oven and place clams on top, do not cover, return to oven for 5-8 minutes. Serve in same pan.

Submitted by: Michael Mastrogiuseppe, Local Winner — Bradenton Herald

Favorite thing about this recipe: I got the recipe in Spain.

Healthy Harvest Rotini

- 1 cup red lentil rotini or fusilli pasta (such as Trader Joe's Sedanini)
- 2 1/2 cups butternut or honeynut squash, cubed
- 1 Tbsp olive oil
- 1/2 onion, chopped
- 2 cloves garlic, minced
- 2 links hot Italian sausage or plant-based sausage, sliced
- 1/4 tsp dried thyme
- Salt, pepper and red pepper flakes to taste
- Parmesan cheese, grated, for serving

Total time: 30 minutes
Serves 4

Heat water for pasta. Cook as directed and drain.

Place squash cubes in covered, microwave-safe container with small amount of water and microwave for 3-4 minutes or until mostly soft. Drain.

In a large skillet, saute onion and garlic in olive oil until slightly softened. Add sausage and cook, stirring occasionally, until sausage is heated through.

Add squash and thyme, stir to combine. Simmer on low heat for a few minutes.

Add cooked pasta to skillet; stir to combine. Mash the squash slightly to create a creamy coating for the pasta; season with salt, pepper and red pepper flakes to taste. Drizzle with a little olive oil and top with grated Parmesan cheese, if desired.

Submitted by: Lisa Schneider, Local Winner — Centre Daily Times

Favorite thing about this recipe: Quick, economical and tastes rich and satisfying without the calories.

RZB's Red Beans-N-Rice

- 1/8 cup olive oil
- 1 large or 2 small onions, diced
- 1 clove garlic (or more), crushed
- 3-6 small green chili peppers from Texas Pete Green Pepper Sauce, finely chopped
- 1/4 cup jalapeño peppers (pickled is an option, drain the juice well), coarsely chopped
- 1 Tbsp crushed red pepper
- 8 oz Pace Hot Picante Sauce (or substitute with RO*TEL Diced Tomatoes & Green Chilies, 10 oz can)
- 1 ham steak with the bone, fat removed and cubed; save bone
- 1 1/2 packs Hillshire Farm Smoked Sausage, sliced
- 1 Tbsp red pepper
- 1 Tbsp white pepper
- 4-6 Tbsp chili powder
- Two 14.5-oz cans fire-roasted diced tomatoes
- 2 cans kidney beans (one dark red, one light red)
- 1 can whole corn, drained
- 2 cans Campbell's Cream of Mushroom Soup

Total time: 1 hour, 30 minutes
Serves 8

In a heavy stainless or aluminum pot, heat olive oil on medium to medium-high heat. Saute the onions, garlic, jalapeño peppers and the ham bone. Halfway through sauteing (borderline browning), also add the chili peppers, the crushed red pepper and Pace Hot Picante Sauce, and bring it to a simmer, reducing until it is close to a paste.

Add meat and cover with the spices. Cover and simmer on low medium heat for about 15 minutes, no stirring.

Add the fire-roasted tomatoes. Uncover, raise the heat and stir; if soupy, continue to simmer to reduce the sauce. Continue stirring and lower the heat; cook the flavor into the meat.

Add the beans, corn and mushroom soup, and up to 1 can of water for desired consistency. Stir and cover on low heat for about 30 minutes — the longer the better.

Serve over rice. Delicious with cornbread on the side.

Note

I like mixing 2 parts jasmine rice to 1 part brown rice. Cook per directions — never use instant!

Submitted by: Robert Bouck, Local Winner — The Charlotte Observer

Favorite thing about this recipe: You can make it your own easily.

Deconstructed Eggplant Cannelloni with Cashew Crema

photo on page 85

- 1 medium eggplant, cut into bite-size cubes
- 1 Tbsp olive oil
- 1/2 tsp salt
- 1/2 cup penne pasta, dry
- 3 cups spinach leaves, roughly chopped
- 1/2 cup (packed) fresh basil leaves, roughly chopped
- 1/3 cups freshly roasted pine nuts (optional)

Sauce

- 1 Tbsp olive oil
- 2 large cloves garlic, chopped
- 1 small-to-medium red onion, diced, about 1 1/3 cup
- 14.5-oz can fire-roasted tomatoes
- 1/2 tsp Sriracha sauce
- 1/2 cup water
- 1 tsp thyme, dried
- 1 tsp oregano, dried
- 1/4 tsp black pepper

Crema

- 1 cup raw, unsalted cashews
- 2 Tbsp fresh lemon juice
- 1/2 tsp garlic powder
- 1/4 tsp salt
- 2 Tbsp nutritional yeast
- 1/2 cup water

Total time: 1 hour, 10 minutes
Serves 4-6

Heat oven to 400 F. Cover cashews with boiling water and set aside.

Line baking sheet with parchment paper and place cubed eggplant on it. Toss with olive oil and salt. Bake for 15 minutes. Set aside and lower oven temperature to 350 F.

Make the sauce: Add olive oil to skillet on medium heat. Add garlic and onion and saute until fragrant, 2-3 minutes. Add tomatoes, Sriracha, water, thyme, oregano and pepper. Simmer uncovered for 10 minutes.

Make the crema: Rinse and drain cashews. Add to food processor or high-speed blender with lemon juice, garlic powder, salt, nutritional yeast and water. Process until smooth.

Cook penne pasta according to package directions and drain. In a 9x13-inch or loaf-size baking dish, combine tomato sauce mixture into drained pasta. Stir in spinach and fresh basil.

Use a soup spoon to drop crema on top. Use a knife to roughly marble mixture. Cover with foil and bake 10 minutes. Remove foil and bake 5 more minutes. Sprinkle with roasted pine nuts if using.

Submitted by: Stacy Renee Lucas, Local Winner — The Fresno Bee

Favorite thing about this recipe: I love the festive holiday colors, and I really love the fact that I can have everything I like about Eggplant Cannelloni without spending hours in the kitchen. I was inspired when I had a deconstructed eggplant Parmesan and decided to do the same.

Dr Pepper Pulled Brisket

photo on page 85

- 4 lbs beef brisket, first cut
- 1 Tbsp kosher salt
- 1 Tbsp black pepper
- 1/2 small onion, chopped
- 4 cloves garlic, chopped
- 2 chipotle chiles in adobo sauce
- 1/2 cup Dr Pepper, not diet, preferably made with cane sugar
- 1 cup ketchup
- 2 Tbsp yellow mustard
- 1 Tbsp molasses
- 1 tsp Worcestershire sauce
- 2 tsp smoked paprika

Total time: 6 hours
Serves 8

Heat oven to 250 F. Sprinkle brisket on both sides with salt and pepper, place in a roasting pan fat side up, and allow to come to room temperature.

Make the sauce: In a blender or food processor, place the onion, garlic, chipotle chiles, 1/4 cup of the Dr Pepper, ketchup, mustard, molasses, Worcestershire, smoked paprika and ground cloves. Puree until smooth, and add salt and pepper to taste.

Lift up the brisket and pour 1/2 the sauce into the bottom of the pan. Place the brisket, fat side up, on top of the sauce, pour in the remaining 1/4 cup of Dr Pepper, then pour the remaining sauce over the brisket.

Cover pan tightly with foil. Place the pan in the oven and cook 5 hours (or 1 hour and 15 minutes per pound). Test it to see if it's fork tender. If you can easily stick a fork into then it's done. If not, continue to cook it until it is fork tender, checking it every 20 minutes.

Once done, remove the pan from the oven, remove foil and gently lift the brisket out of the pan into a large mixing bowl or baking dish, retaining the juices. Allow the brisket to rest for 30 minutes.

Pour the roasting pan juices into a pot, turn the heat up to high and reduce in half, about 20 to 30 minutes. (I don't strain the fat, but feel free to do so if you prefer.)

Once the pan juices have reduced and the brisket has rested, shred the brisket in the large bowl with two forks. Pour the sauce over the brisket and toss well. Add salt and pepper to taste. Optional: Add another tsp of smoked paprika to taste.

Serve with warm tortillas and salsa for tacos, put it on buns, use it for nachos or throw some into a bowl of queso.

Submitted by: Rebecca Taylor, Local Winner — Fort Worth Star-Telegram

Favorite thing about this recipe: Tender, delicious, versatile.

Camp Dish

- 3 Tbsp butter
- 1 green bell pepper, chopped
- 1 small onion, chopped
- 1 lb ground beef
- 1 can tomato sauce
- 1 can light red or dark kidney beans, drained
- 1/2 tsp salt
- 1/4 tsp paprika
- 1 tsp Worcestershire sauce

Total time: 40 minutes
Serves 4-6

Saute pepper and onion in butter, add beef and brown lightly. Add other ingredients and simmer 25 minutes.

Submitted by: Carol McBride, Local Winner — The Island Packet

Favorite thing about this recipe: It is easy, quick and wonderful with a salad and French bread.

Mom's Cheesy Spaghetti Casserole

- 1/4 lb bacon, cut into small pieces and fried
- 1 large onion, chopped
- 1 lb ground beef
- 8-oz can tomato sauce
- 1/2 tsp garlic salt
- 1/8 tsp pepper
- 4-oz can sliced mushrooms, drained
- 12-oz package thin spaghetti
- 1 cup shredded cheddar cheese
- 1/2 cup of shredded Provolone cheese

Total time: 1 hour
Serves 4

Heat oven to 375 F. Fry the bacon until brown, drain off grease and set aside. To the same pan, add onion and beef, cook until meat is brown. Mix in the tomato sauce, seasonings, mushrooms and chopped cooked bacon. Simmer 15 minutes.

Cook the spaghetti and drain. In a large pan combine the spaghetti and the sauce. In a medium bowl, combine the two cheeses. Place 1/2 of the spaghetti mixture in a buttered 2-quart casserole dish. Sprinkle with 1/2 the cheese. Repeat with the rest of the spaghetti and sauce mixture, cover with remaining cheese. Bake for 20 minutes. Serve with breadsticks and salad.

Submitted by: Ellen Caristo, Local Winner — Tri-City Herald

Favorite thing about this recipe: Easy, tasty and my husband loves it.

Butternut Squash Lasagna with Italian Deer Sausage

- 1 large or 2 small butternut squash
- Salt and pepper
- Garlic powder
- Olive oil
- 15-oz container ricotta cheese
- 1 egg
- Packaged shredded Italian cheese blend
- Fresh basil
- 1 large sweet onion, diced
- 1/2 pint baby portobello mushrooms, chopped (medium-to-large chunks)
- 1 lb mild Italian deer sausage (or Italian pork sausage), ground or casings removed
- 1 large clove of garlic, minced
- Fresh Parmesan cheese
- Baby spinach (optional)
- No-boil (oven-ready) lasagna noodles

Total time: 2 hours, 30 minutes
Serves 6

Heat oven onto 350 F. Stab the squash a few times with a fork. Place in the microwave for 4-6 minutes. This makes it much easier to cut in half. Remove them from the microwave and allow to cool. Cut in half lengthwise, scoop out the seeds, and lay flesh side up on a sheet pan covered with foil. Generously cover with olive oil, salt, pepper and garlic powder. Place in the oven for about 45 minutes.

In a medium bowl, whisk ricotta and egg. Stir in 1 to 1 1/2 cups of shredded Italian cheese blend with pinch of salt and pepper. Take a small handful of fresh basil, julienne it, and mix it into the cheese mixture. Set aside.

In a large pan on medium heat, add olive oil and saute a diced sweet onion and chopped baby portobello mushrooms. Once the onions and mushrooms are aromatic, add in sausage (or none at all) and brown it. When the meat is mostly browned, add garlic to the pan.

By now, the butternut squash should be ready. It should be soft enough that you can easily scoop out spoonfuls — if it is not, place it back in the oven for 5 minutes. Allow time to cool! Do not worry if the skin gets a little burnt. Keep oven at 350 F, and in the same pan as meat, onions and mushrooms, add butternut squash by the spoonful. It should be easy to stir. Add more salt and pepper if necessary. At this stage, if you'd like to add spinach, grab 2-3 handfuls and fold it into the squash and meat mixture so that it begins to wilt.

Prepare the baking dish with butter or oil. Add a small amount of the squash and meat mixture to coat the bottom and lay down a layer of pasta. Next, add 1/2 the ricotta and cheese mixture, then 1/2 the meat and squash mixture, then more pasta — repeat! Depending on the depth of your pan, be generous with your layers. Sprinkle in extra Parmesan with every layer.

Sprinkle more shredded cheese and fresh grated Parmesan on top, and cover with foil. Let the lasagna bake covered for 30-45 minutes. Baking times vary by oven or pan depth — wait until it begins bubbling in the pan. Remove the foil and bake for another 10-15 minutes — just long enough to crisp and to brown the extra cheese on top.

Let the lasagna rest on top of the stove for at least 30 minutes. This meal can be easily made vegetarian or gluten free!

Submitted by: Virginia Ariail, Local Winner — The State

Favorite thing about this recipe: It's a perfect fall weather dish with delicious smells that fill your house; it is a hearty meal that can be made inexpensively and can be the best leftovers the next day if any is left!

Broccoli, Chicken and Rice Casserole

- 2 chicken breasts, chopped
- 1/2 tsp salt
- 1/2 tsp onion powder
- 1 tsp pepper
- 1 lb broccoli
- 1/2 medium onion, chopped
- 1 cup Sargento Shredded 4 State Cheddar Cheese
- 1/4 cup cooked rice
- 1 can Campbell's Cream of Mushroom Soup
- 1/2 tsp garlic powder
- 1/4 tsp Slap Ya Mama Cajun Seasoning

Total time: 1 hour
Serves 2-4

Heat oven to 350 F. In a pan, cook chicken with a dash of salt, onion powder and pepper.

Remove chicken when done and set aside. Save the chicken broth.

In the same pan, cook broccoli and onion in the leftover chicken broth until about half done (still crunchy).

Let vegetables rest 10 minutes.

To pan, add chopped chicken breast, 1/2 cup cheese, rice, creamed soup, garlic powder and Slap Ya Mama seasoning, and mix all together.

Place in an 8x8 pan and bake for 30 minutes.

Submitted by: Deborah Thompson, Lexington Herald-Leader

Favorite thing about this recipe: All-in-one main dish.

Shrimp and Mussel Ravioli Bake with Creamy Tomato Sauce

Creamy Tomato Sauce

- 2 Tbsp olive oil
- 1 small yellow onion, finely diced
- 1 small red bell pepper, finely diced
- 4 cloves garlic, pressed
- 2 Tbsp tomato paste
- 2 Tbsp fresh thyme leaves, can be removed from stems and finely chopped, or 5-6 whole sprigs
- 2 tsp smoked paprika
- 1 1/2 tsp salt
- 1 tsp freshly ground black pepper
- 1 Tbsp herbes de Provence
- 1 cup crushed tomatoes
- 2 Tbsp balsamic vinegar
- 1 cup heavy cream
- 1 large bunch basil, about 10 oz, finely chopped

Ravioli Base

- Two 10-oz packages spinach and ricotta ravioli (such as Giovanni Rana)

Seafood

- 2 Tbsp butter
- 1 lb uncooked shrimp, peeled, deveined and tails removed
- 1 lb mussel meat
- 1/8 tsp salt
- 1/8 tsp freshly ground black pepper

Topping

- 2 Tbsp capers
- 1/2 cup ricotta cheese
- 2 1/2 cups grated mozzarella cheese

Total time: 1 hour
Serves 6-8

Heat oven to 350 F.

In a large frying pan over medium, heat olive oil and add finely diced onion and red bell pepper. Cook until pepper is tender and onion begins to turn translucent. Onion should not brown.

Add in pressed garlic cloves, tomato paste, thyme, smoked paprika, herbes de Provence, salt and pepper. Simmer for 2 minutes, stirring constantly.

Add in crushed tomatoes and balsamic vinegar. Stir and simmer for 2 minutes.

Add the heavy cream and basil. Simmer about 5 minutes over medium heat, so flavors combine, then set aside.

For ravioli, heat about 8 cups of water in a large Dutch oven and bring to a rolling boil. Add both bags of ravioli, stirring occasionally, until al dente. This should take about 5 minutes. Drain ravioli and set aside.

Place butter in a large frying pan over medium heat. Melt butter and allow it to get a bit brown, then add shrimp and mussel meat. Season with salt and pepper and cook until shrimp begin to turn a pale pink, about 3 minutes.

To assemble, put ravioli in a 9x13 baking dish. Pour sauce and about 1 cup of seafood mixture over and toss gently to until ravioli is coated. Add ricotta cheese and capers, dispersing in small spoonfuls over the dish. Toss gently.

Spread remaining seafood mixture over the top of the bake and top with 2 1/2 cups mozzarella cheese. Place in preheated oven and bake, uncovered, for 40 minutes until lightly golden brown and bubbly. Let stand for 15 minutes.

Submitted by: Sarah Sheven, Local Winner — The Sacramento Bee

Favorite thing about this recipe: How the creamy tomato sauce combines with the shrimp and mussels.

Vivid Potatoes and Chicken

Mashed Potatoes

- 1-1 1/2 lb mini blue potatoes, cubed
- 1/3 cup Parmesan cheese, grated
- Salt and pepper

Topping

- 1 cup shredded kale
- 1/2 cup matchstick carrots
- 2 Tbsp white wine vinegar
- 1 tsp balsamic vinegar
- Olive oil
- Salt and pepper

Chicken

- 2 boneless, skinless chicken breasts
- 1 tsp turmeric
- 1/4 tsp cayenne
- Vegetable oil
- Salt and pepper

Total time: 40 minutes
Serves 2-4

Boil the potatoes and drain. Add the Parmesan and mash them. Salt and pepper to taste.

Shred the kale and break up the carrots slightly. Stir in the vinegars and olive oil, then add salt and pepper.

Lightly rub the turmeric, cayenne and seasonings on the chicken breasts. Put vegetable oil in a grill pan and heat. Lay the chicken on the pan and cook it fully.

Serve by placing the chicken on a bed of mashed potatoes and topping it with the kale topping. Enjoy!

Submitted by: Susan Walker, Local Winner — The Telegraph (Macon)

Favorite thing about this recipe: The vivid flavors and eye-catching colors.

Tex-Mex Meatloaf

- 1 lb ground beef
- 2 eggs
- 1 cup breadcrumbs, plain
- 1/4 cup Parmesan cheese
- 1/4 cup onions, chopped
- 8 oz chunky salsa, mild

Total time: 1 hour, 25 minutes
Serves 6-8

Heat oven to 350 F.

In a large bowl, combine all ingredients. Place in lightly greased 5x9 loaf pan. Bake for 60 minutes. Let stand 10 minutes.

Submitted by: Linda Rothrauff, Sun Herald

Favorite thing about this recipe: The flavor.

Oven Fried Fish

photo on page 88
- 2/3 cup yellow cornmeal
- 1/3 cup all-purpose flour
- 1/4 tsp Creole seasoning
- 1/8 tsp cayenne pepper
- 1/2 tsp salt
- 1/2 cup prepared yellow mustard
- 1/2 tsp Tabasco hot sauce
- 1 lb tilapia fillets
- Nonstick cooking spray

Total time: 50 minutes
Serves 2-4

Heat oven to 375 F.

Mix the cornmeal, flour and spices in a small bowl. In separate bowl, mix the mustard and hot sauce.

Slather both sides of each fillet with the mustard mixture and then roll it in the cornmeal mixture until well coated.

Place fillets (do not stack) on baking sheet sprayed with nonstick cooking spray. Let fillets rest at room temp for about 10 minutes. Lightly spray the top of each fillet with nonstick cooking spray.

Bake for about 25 minutes, until fish is flaky and done. Cooking time varies depending on thickness of fish fillet.

Submitted by: Eva King, Sun Herald

Favorite thing about this recipe: It reminds me of childhood summers, camping on Black Creek with my family and eating freshly caught fried fish. This is a healthier version of that childhood favorite.

Terrebonne Cajun Cabbage

photo on page 91

- 1/4 cup canola oil
- 16 oz Hickory smoked bacon, cut into 1-inch pieces
- 1 yellow onion, finely chopped
- 1 green bell pepper, finely chopped
- 2 celery stalks, finely chopped
- 2 heads cabbage, chopped into quarters with the cores removed
- 1 Tbsp Tony Chachere's Original Creole Seasoning
- 1 tsp black pepper
- 2 packages Chisesi's Pride seasoned ham
- 2 packages Zatarain's Cajun Style Smoked Sausage, cut in 1/2-inch slices
- 1 Chisesi's smoked ham shank
- 8 cups water
- 3 cups Zatarain's long grain rice

Total time: 3 hours
Serves 12

In a 20-quart pot, add oil, chopped bacon. Brown bacon, then add chopped veggies and cook until onions are soft. Add cabbage, seasonings, meat and water.

Place lid bring to boil then simmer for 3 hours, stirring occasionally.

Cook rice according to instructions. Serve with rice.

Submitted by: Troy Terrebonne, Sun Herald

Favorite thing about this recipe: Easy and tastes delicious.

Turtle Soup

- 2 tsp butter
- 1 apple, peeled and chopped
- 1 onion, chopped
- 2 tsp curry powder
- 4 cups chicken broth
- 1/2 cup uncooked rice
- 1 cup cream
- 1 large zucchini, grated, drain well

Total time: 1 hour, 30 minutes
Serves 4

Melt butter and saute apple and onion together until tender, about 2 minutes.

Sprinkle on curry powder. Stir until blended. Pour in chicken broth, grated zucchini and rice. Cook until rice is tender, on medium heat for 30 minutes. Add cream and heat through.

Submitted by: Dorinda Mattson, The Bellingham Herald

Favorite thing about this recipe: The taste.

Speckled Trout a la Meunier

photo on page 89

- 4 speckled trout fillets
- Salt and pepper
- 1 cup flour
- 6 Tbsp butter, divided
- 4 Tbsp olive oil, divided
- 1 small shallot, minced
- 1/2 cup white wine
- 2 Tbsp lemon juice
- Parsley
- Thyme
- 6 oz baby spinach
- 12 cherry tomatoes
- 8 oz cooked pasta

Total time 30-40 minutes
Serves 4

Heat oven to 200 F.

Salt and pepper trout, then dredge in flour. Saute in 3 Tbsp each butter and olive oil, 2 1/2 to 3 minutes per side. Transfer to oven safe dish and keep warm in oven.

Add 3 Tbsp butter and 1 Tbsp olive oil to pan and saute shallot for about 30 seconds. Add wine, lemon juice, spinach and cherry tomatoes. Cook just until spinach is wilted and tomatoes start to blister. Add the thyme and parsley to the sauce during the last 15-20 seconds of cooking. Turn off heat and add cooked pasta of your choice. Serve with trout.

Submitted by: Gail Jordan, Sun Herald

Favorite thing about this recipe: Beautiful and delicious.

Sausage Souffle

- 6 slices white bread
- 1 package of Hillshire Farm Smoked Sausage
- 8 eggs
- 2 cups milk
- 1/2 tsp salt
- 1/2 tsp mustard powder
- Green onion, chopped
- 1 cup sharp cheese, grated

Total time: 24 hours
Prep/baking time: 1 hour, 15 minutes
Serves 6-8

Make ahead: Decrust and finely cube bread, place in buttered 9x13 baking dish.

Add sausages. Beat eggs with salt and mustard. Add milk and blend. Pour over cubed bread, top with onions and cheese. Cover and place in the refrigerator overnight.

Heat oven to 325 F. Bake 45-50 minutes.

Submitted by: Carolyn Blakeway, The Bellingham Herald

Favorite thing about this recipe: Prepare the day before.

Irie Enchilada Casserole

- 1 sweet potato, cut into 1/2-inch rounds
- 1 medium yellow onion, diced
- 1 bunch kale, chard or other leafy green, cleaned and chopped
- 1 1/2 cups frozen corn
- 2 tsp cumin
- Salt and pepper
- 22-oz can green enchilada sauce
- 12 corn tortillas
- 4 cups cheddar cheese
- Red chili flakes (optional)

Total time: 1 hour, 30 minutes
Serves 8

Heat oven to 375 F.

Steam cut sweet potato until soft, either in microwave with a small amount of water or in steamer.

In large pan, saute onions until soft, then add sweet potatoes, kale, frozen corn, cumin, salt and pepper to taste. Cook until kale is wilted.

In large casserole dish, pour in a bit of enchilada sauce to cover bottom.

Dip tortillas into enchilada sauce, then add single layer of tortillas (break some in half for straight edges to go against sides)

Add all filling, spreading evenly across dish. Sprinkle 3/4 of cheddar cheese on top of veggies.

Add another single layer of tortillas, dipping in enchilada sauce first. Top with remaining enchilada sauce. Sprinkle remaining cheese over top. Add sprinkles of red chili flakes if desired.

Cook in oven for about 30 minutes or until bubbling.

Submitted by: Jenna Deane, The Bellingham Herald

Favorite thing about this recipe: Easy, delicious and filling vegetarian enchiladas.

Braised Beef Brisket with Brown Gravy

Brisket

- 4 lbs beef brisket
- 1 cup dry red wine
- 3 cups boiling water

Marinade

- 1 Tbsp kosher salt
- 1/2 tsp coarsely ground pepper
- 1 Tbsp tomato paste
- 1 Tbsp olive oil
- 1/4 cup Dijon mustard
- 1/4 cup balsamic vinegar
- 1/4 cup garlic, finely minced

Gravy

- Chilled pan juices, fat removed
- 4 Tbsp butter
- 4 Tbsp all-purpose flour
- Minced flat-leaf parsley

Total time: 2 days
Prep/baking time: 4 hours
Serves 8

Day One: Marinate and Braise

Using a sharp knife, trim the excess fat and any stray bits. Be careful to leave 1/8-to-1/4-inch of the fat layer. Rinse the brisket, pat dry with paper towel. Using the knife, pierce each side of the brisket 20-30 times in an all-over pattern; this will enhance absorption of the marinade.

Combine the marinade ingredients in a medium bowl and stir into a smooth paste. Smear the lean side of the meat with 1/2 of the marinade, and place the meat marinade-side down in the center of a baking dish. Smear the remaining marinade on the fat-side of the brisket. Cover loosely with plastic wrap being careful not to disturb the layer of marinade. Let rest at room temperature for one hour.

Heat oven to 375 F.

Uncover the brisket and place in the upper third of the oven; roast uncovered for 30 minutes. Remove from the oven and reduce the heat to 325 F. Combine the wine and boiling water in a heat-proof measuring cup; pour into the pan, being careful not to disturb the meat's marinade coating. Cover tightly with heavy aluminum foil lined with a piece of parchment paper. Let the brisket braise in the lower third of the oven for 3 hours. Do not uncover at any time.

Remove the brisket from the oven and let rest at room temperature, for 1-2 hours. Again, do not uncover while resting. Finally, unwrap the brisket and remove the meat from the pan juices. The meat will have shrunk considerably and there will be 2-3 cups of dark, greasy drippings. When cool enough to handle, place the whole brisket in an airtight container and refrigerate overnight. Important: Do not slice yet.

Using a rubber spatula, squeegee all of the pan juices — grease and all — into an airtight container and refrigerate overnight.

Day Two: Make the Gravy and Serve

Heat oven to 375 F.

Take meat from the fridge and slice against the grain into 4-inch slices. Arrange the sliced brisket in a casserole dish and sprinkle with a little water; cover and place in the preheated oven while you make the gravy.

Take the chilled pan juices from the fridge, remove the solid fat layer and discard. The remainder will be dark, potent and (possibly) gelatinous. Pour through a strainer to remove bits and sediment; this will not diminish the flavor. On low heat, melt the butter in a medium saucepan.

When the foam subsides, stir in the flour and cook the roux for 3-4 minutes. Whisk in the pan drippings. If necessary, you can dilute to taste with a little boiling water, beef stock or red wine. Reduce heat and simmer until thickened. Taste and season, if necessary. Garnish the brisket with minced parsley and serve side-by-side with the brown gravy.

Submitted by: Kim Cunningham, The Bellingham Herald

Favorite thing about this recipe: Delicious modern version of a traditional comfort food.

Bean Tortilla

photo on page 82

- 14-oz bag great northern beans, white beans (or 3 cans white beans, rinsed)
- 1 short rib, bone in
- 4 Tbsp olive oil
- 1 Tbsp butter
- 8 oz diced ham
- 2 small chorizo links, chopped
- 1 onion, chopped
- 4 cloves garlic, chopped
- 1/4 green pepper, chopped
- 1/4 cup Jack Daniel's (or other whiskey)
- 8-oz can tomato sauce
- 1/4 cup reserved bean broth

Total time: 1 hour, 10 minutes
Serves 6-8

In a pressure cooker, place beans and short rib in water and cook for 25 minutes. If not using pressure cooker, use the canned, rinsed beans.

Heat oven to 350 F.

Remove short rib meat from pressure cooker. Remove bone and chop meat.

In an oven-proof skillet, add oil and butter over medium heat. Add the ham, chorizo, short rib meat, onion, garlic and green pepper. Cook for 5 minutes. Add the whiskey and tomato sauce. Cook additional 5 minutes. Drain the beans and add the beans to the sauce followed by the bean broth. When all is well mixed, place in oven 25 minutes.

Serve over rice.

Submitted by: Nancy Wilson, Local Winner — Miami Herald

Favorite thing about this recipe: The flavor.

Vegetable-Beef Barley Soup

- 2-3 cups leftover pot roast meat, chopped
- 1 1/2 cups onion, chopped
- 2 Tbsp garlic, chopped (Tip: buy in a jar)
- 14 cups water
- 4 Tbsp Better Than Bouillon beef flavor
- 28-oz can diced tomatoes
- 3 bay leaves
- 1 Tbsp Italian seasoning
- 2 tsp salt
- 12-oz package Kroger Vegetable Soup Mix
- 12-oz package frozen mixed vegetables
- 2 celery stalks, diced
- 2 cups cabbage, chopped (or pre-packaged coleslaw mix)
- 3/4 cup uncooked barley
- 1/4 cup Pace Original Picante Sauce, medium
- 1 can kidney beans
- 1/3 cup red wine
- 1 cup chopped zucchini
- 1 cup chopped cauliflower
- Leftover beef gravy (if so desired)

Total time: 8 hours, 25 minutes
Serves 10-12

Add all the ingredients to slow cooker and set on high. After 1 hour, turn down to low and cook for about 8 hours.

Submitted by: Laina Jansma, The Bellingham Herald

Favorite thing about this recipe: It's very nutritious and the combination of Better Than Bouillon, tomatoes, garlic and the seasonings gives it an outstanding flavor!

My Thank You Casserole

- 5 potatoes, sliced
- 1 lb ground beef, raw
- 1 medium onion, sliced
- 1 can vegetable beef soup
- 1 can cream of mushroom soup

Total time: 1 hour, 45 minutes
Serves 5-6

Heat oven to 350 F. Put sliced potatoes in bottom of a greased casserole pan. Break meat over potatoes. Put sliced onion over meat. Add vegetable beef soup. Add cream of mushroom soup. Cover tightly with foil. Bake 1 1/2 hours.

Submitted by: Corinne Mewes, Belleville News-Democrat

Favorite thing about this recipe: This recipe is comfort food at its best. It's been a fixture at my own table for many years. It also makes a great dish to take to a neighbor in need or to say "thank you" with.

Mama Lou Lou's Chili

- 1 Tbsp oil
- 2 lbs ground beef
- 1 medium onion, diced
- 46-oz can tomato juice
- Two 14.5-oz cans Just For Chili Diced Tomatoes
- 14.5-oz can petite diced tomatoes
- Two 15.5-oz cans chili beans, mild
- 1/2 cup chili powder
- 2 Tbsp Mexican chili powder
- 1 Tbsp cumin
- 2 Tbsp sugar

Total time: 1 hour
Serves 8-10

Add oil to large skillet. Add ground beef and onion. Heat on medium-high heat until meat browns and onions are soft (approximately 6 to 7 minutes). Drain fat. Add tomato juice, Just For Chili Diced Tomatoes and petite diced tomatoes, chili beans, chili powder, Mexican chili powder, cumin and sugar. Stir together and bring to a boil. Simmer on medium-low heat for 30 to 45 minutes.

Submitted by: Mary Lou Wittenauer, Belleville News-Democrat

Favorite thing about this recipe: It brings the whole family together at meal time.

Hunter's Finger Steaks

photo on page 86

- 2-3 lbs elk, venison or beef round steak
- 4 eggs, beaten
- 2 tsp garlic salt
- 2 tsp lemon pepper
- 2-3 sleeves saltine crackers
- Ranch dressing or Asian sweet chili sauce for dipping

Total time: 2-3 hours
Serves 6-8

Cut meat into bite size pieces. Tip: meat is easier to cut if partially frozen.

In a large bowl, combine eggs, garlic salt and lemon pepper. Marinate meat in egg mixture for 2 to 3 hours at room temperature, refrigerate if longer.

Heat oil in skillet or Fry Daddy to 350 F.

Crush saltines. Roll meat in saltines and fry for about 2 minutes until golden brown, do not overcook as meat will dry out. Remove with slotted spoon to paper towel-lined dish and salt to taste. Serve with dipping sauce.

Submitted by: LaFaye Farris, Idaho Statesman

Favorite thing about this recipe: Being an Idahoan, I was raised on wild game. My grandsons love this recipe because it showcases their hunting skills. These are good cold too!

Eggplant Mozzarella

- 2 medium eggplants
- 2 Tbsp salt
- 1 cup olive oil
- 16 oz round mozzarella cheese, sliced into 1/2-inch pieces
- Favorite spaghetti sauce recipe

Total time: 1 hour, 45 minutes
Serves 6-8

Trim off ends of each eggplant, do not peel. Slice each eggplant into 3/4-inch slices. Lay slices in 13x9 inch casserole pan. Sprinkle the salt on both sides of eggplant slices and allow to sit for about an hour. When ready to continue, gently wipe the salt off the eggplant slices and pat dry.

Heat oven to 325 F.

In frying pan, add 1/2 cup olive oil and heat on medium. Place each slice of eggplant into oil. Eggplant absorbs oil rapidly so add more oil as needed. Cook and turn until both sides of each piece is slightly browned.

Place slices back into casserole pan. Cover each eggplant slice with a slice of mozzarella. Pour spaghetti sauce over all. Bake in oven for 45 minutes or until cheese is well melted.

Submitted by: Sandy Harris, Idaho Statesman

Favorite thing about this recipe: Healthy and delicious!

Gluten-Free Oat Bran Waffles with Yogurt Maple Syrup

Waffles

- 1/2 cup rice flour
- 1/2 cup tapioca starch/flour
- 1/2 cup potato starch (not potato flour)
- 1/4 cup coconut flour
- 1/4 cup oat bran
- 1 tsp xanthan gum
- 1 Tbsp granulated sugar
- 4 tsp baking powder
- 1/4 tsp salt
- 2 large eggs
- 1 3/4 cups milk (or dairy-free milk)
- 1/2 cup avocado oil
- 1/2 tsp pure vanilla extract

Syrup

- 1 cup plain yogurt
- 1/4 to 1/3 cup pure maple syrup

Total time: 35 minutes
Serves 4

Waffles

Heat an electric nonstick waffle iron to 400 F.

In a large mixing bowl, combine dry ingredients: rice flour, tapioca starch/flour, potato starch, coconut flour, oat bran, xanthan gum, sugar, baking powder and salt. Stir gently until evenly mixed.

Add eggs, milk, oil and vanilla. Mix just until batter is smooth.

Pour batter onto hot waffle iron (about 1/4 cup per 4-inch waffle). Cook for 7 or 8 minutes, until golden.

Syrup

Whisk together plain yogurt and maple syrup in a small pitcher or bowl until smooth and silky. Serve with waffles.

Submitted by: Anita Flora, Idaho Statesman

Favorite thing about this recipe: It's gluten-free, contains extra fiber, the yogurt gives an extra dimension to the maple syrup and it's delicious!

Minestrone

- 2 Tbsp olive oil
- 2 celery stalks, chopped
- 1 carrot, chopped
- 1 onion, chopped
- 1 clove garlic, minced
- 1/2 tsp rosemary
- 2 oz prosciutto, finely chopped
- 1 lb ground beef
- 14-oz can crushed tomatoes
- 1 cup red wine
- 2 red potatoes, cubed
- 4 cups beef broth
- 14-oz can kidney beans, rinsed and drained
- 14-oz can garbanzo beans, rinsed and drained
- 1/3 cup small pasta shells
- 1/3 cup Romano cheese, grated
- 1/2 cup parsley, minced
- 1 clove garlic, minced
- 1 Tbsp lemon zest

Total time: 1 hour
Serves 6-8

In a large pot, heat the oil over medium heat. Add celery, carrot, onion and garlic, stirring until the mixture begins to brown.

Add the rosemary and cook 10 seconds. Add the prosciutto and the ground beef, cook breaking beef until is no longer pink.

Add the tomatoes with their juices, wine and potatoes and simmer for 10 minutes. Add the beef broth and the beans, bring the mixture to a rolling boil and sprinkle pasta over the surface. Simmer the soup, partially covered for 20 minutes, stirring frequently. Season with salt and pepper.

In a small bowl mix together the Romano cheese, parsley, garlic and lemon zest. Serve with soup as a garnish.

Submitted by: Gloria Murphy, Idaho Statesman

Favorite thing about this recipe: It's very comforting.

One-Pot Stuffed Pepper Soup

- 1 lb ground beef
- 1 large onion, diced
- 2 cloves garlic, minced
- 2 large green bell peppers, chopped
- 4 cups beef broth
- 1/2 cup tomato sauce
- 14.5-oz can diced tomatoes
- 1 1/2 tsp salt
- 1/2 tsp ground pepper
- 1 tsp oregano
- 1/2 tsp basil
- 1/2 tsp thyme
- 3-4 drops stevia
- 1/2 cup brown rice, uncooked

Total time: 40 minutes
Serves 6-8

In large pan, brown beef. Add veggies and cook a few minutes. Add rest of ingredients (through stevia) and bring to a boil. Add rice and simmer, covered, for 15-20 minutes. Taste to adjust seasoning.

If desired, for a heartier soup, add 1 package of frozen gnocchi during the last 5-6 minutes of cooking (such as Trader Joe's Kale Gnocchi). Best made a day ahead.

Submitted by: Lisa Schneider, Centre Daily Times

Favorite thing about this recipe: Hearty, healthy, delicious — and only one pot to wash!

Potato Something Else

photo on page 91

- 6-7 medium potatoes, diced
- 1 package onion soup or 2 cups bouillon
- 1/2-1 lb hamburger (or 1/2 lb ground sausage and 1/2 lb hamburger)
- 1/2-1 onion, diced
- 2-3 celery stalks, diced
- 1 can cream of "something" soup
- 1/2-1 cup grated cheese, divided (your choice of cheese)

Total time: 1 hour
Serves 8

Heat oven to 350 F.

Put diced potatoes in the bottom of casserole pan, put pan in the oven while preparing remaining ingredients.

In large skillet, brown meat with soup or bouillon and add the onion and celery. Mix cream of "something" soup into meat mixture and pour over the potatoes. Top with 1/2 the cheese.

Bake 35-40 minutes until potatoes are done.

Sprinkle the rest of the cheese over the casserole while hot — let rest 5-10 minutes.

Serve with a salad.

Submitted by: Anieta Tock,
Idaho Statesman

Creamy Turkey and Rice Soup

photo on page 83

- Turkey bones
- 5 cups water
- 1 cup onion, chopped
- 1 cup carrots, chopped
- 1 cup celery, diced
- 2 Tbsp garlic, minced
- 1/2 cup butter, divided
- 2 cups turkey, diced
- 1 1/2 cups cooked rice
- 1/4 tsp each: thyme, marjoram, sage, rosemary
- 3 tsp chicken bouillon
- 1/2 cup flour
- 1 1/2 cups milk
- 1/2 cup cream

Total time: 15 hours
Serves 12

In slow cooker, add turkey bones and 5 cups of water. Cook on low overnight.

Strain broth and pick out any turkey left on bones. Return broth to the slow cooker.

In pan, saute onion, carrots, celery and garlic in 2 Tbsp butter for about 5 minutes. Add to broth. Add diced turkey, cooked rice, thyme, marjoram, sage, rosemary and bouillon.

In same pot, melt 6 Tbsp butter. Add the flour and mix until combined. Add the milk and cream and stir constantly until thickened. Add to slow cooker. Cook on high for 4 more hours.

Submitted by: Beth Banister, Idaho Statesman

Favorite thing about this recipe: It uses extra meat and bones from Thanksgiving turkey!

Quarantine Quiche

- 1 cup cooked basmati rice
- 5 eggs
- 1/2 cup Parmesan cheese, shredded
- 8 oz ground Italian sausage
- 14-oz can sliced mushrooms
- 14-oz can sliced black olives
- 3/4 cup shredded cheddar cheese
- 1 cup (approximate) milk or half-and-half
- 1 Tbsp dried thyme or 1 tsp fresh thyme
- 1 Tbsp of dried dill or 1 tsp of fresh dill

Total time: 1 hour, 30 minutes
Serves 6

Crust

Allow rice to cool to lukewarm. Beat 1 egg by hand and mix with rice and Parmesan cheese. Press mixture into a 9-inch pie plate. There may be slight gaps in the crust but don't worry.

Filling

Heat oven to 350 F. Saute Italian sausage, drain fat and allow to cool. Line the pie plate with the sausage, then mushrooms and olives, top with cheddar cheese. Beat the remaining eggs with the milk or half-and-half, and fill the pie plate to the top. Sprinkle the thyme and dill on top. Bake for 1 hour, until filling and crust are firm to the touch.

Submitted by: Renae Hoff, Idaho Statesman

Favorite thing about this recipe: Everyone who tries this quiche loves it.

Mexican Meatloaf Surprise

- 2 1/2 lbs ground beef, browned
- 1 package taco seasoning mix
- 1 small jar taco sauce (hot or mild, your choice)
- 1 can cream of celery soup
- 1 can cream of mushroom soup
- 1 can refried beans
- 1 large onion, chopped (Tip: cook this with hamburger)
- 3 or 4 jalapeño peppers, chopped (optional)
- 1 1/2 cups minute rice, cooked
- 2 cups tomato juice
- Bag of Doritos (suggest Nacho Cheese), crushed
- 3 cups shredded cheddar cheese

Total time: 40 minutes
Serves 12

Heat oven to 350 F.

In bowl, add first 10 ingredients and mix thoroughly. Layer 1/2 meat mixture in 9x13 pan. Top with 1/2 of the crushed Doritos and 1/2 the cheddar cheese. Layer the remaining meat mixture, Doritos and cheese.

Bake for 20 minutes or until cheese melts.

Submitted by: Judy Williams, Bradenton Herald

Favorite thing about this recipe: Easy to make and everyone I have served it to asks for recipe.

Salmon Sliders

photo on page 89

- 3-4 slices of bacon, warmed
- 3 King's Hawaiian rolls
- 5-7 oz leftover salmon (such as brown sugar glazed)
- 1-3 Tbsp horseradish cream sauce

Total time: 10 minutes
Serves 1

Cook bacon and warm up King's Hawaiian rolls (10-20 seconds in microwave). Place salmon and bacon on roll with horseradish cream to taste.

Submitted by: Anne Ferrando-Klemet, Bradenton Herald

Favorite thing about this recipe: Great way to use leftover salmon!

Shrimp and Blue Cheese Tortilla

photo on page 89

- 4 flour tortillas
- Oil for frying
- 12 cooked shrimp, chilled
- 4 Tbsp cocktail sauce
- 1/2-1 cup chopped mushrooms, divided into 4 equal portions
- 1/2-1 cup chopped red, yellow and orange peppers, divided into 4 equal portions
- 4-8 Tbsp crumbled blue cheese

Total time: 15 minutes
Serves 2-4

Fry the tortillas until they start to get crispy; dry on paper towels.

Assemble each tortilla: Spread out the cocktail sauce on top of the tortilla; lay 4 shrimp on top of the cocktail sauce; add 1 portion of mushrooms and 1 portion of peppers on top of the shrimp; sprinkle 1-2 Tbsp of the blue cheese on top.

Submitted by: Anne Ferrando-Klemet, Bradenton Herald

Favorite thing about this recipe: My husband said shrimp and blue cheese don't go together — until he ate one!

Busy Day Potato Soup

- 2 oz cooked ham, chopped (or sausage)
- 1 quart chicken broth
- 6 Tbsp butter
- 1/2 onion, diced
- 1 lb potatoes, diced
- 3/4 tsp black pepper
- 1/3 cup flour
- 1 cup milk
- Fresh parsley, chopped (optional)

Total time: 20 minutes
Serves 6

Combine ham and chicken broth. Melt 3 Tbsp butter in stockpot, add onions and saute until translucent. Add potatoes and pepper and stir. Cook until potatoes are done. Make a roux with remaining 3 Tbsp butter, flour and milk (warm in microwave). Add to stock and bring back to boil, stirring constantly. Add parsley, if desired, and serve.

Submitted by: Dianne Powell, Bradenton Herald

Favorite thing about this recipe: Comforting, filling, satisfying and inexpensive.

Easy Spicy Orange Chicken

photo on page 90

- 1/2 cup orange juice
- 1/2 cup Stubb's Original Bar-B-Que Sauce (other kinds are ok, but this is what gives it the perfect sweet and spicy taste)
- 1 Tbsp low-sodium soy sauce
- 2 Tbsp brown sugar
- 1 1/4 lb boneless chicken tenders, cut into cubes
- 3/4 cup flour (can use white or whole wheat flour)
- 3 Tbsp vegetable or olive oil

Total time: 30 minutes
Serves 4

In mixing bowl, combine orange juice, barbecue sauce, soy sauce and brown sugar, and set aside.

In a gallon-size zip-close bag, add flour and chicken cubes. Shake until well coated. Remove chicken with kitchen tongs and shake off extra flour.

In a large nonstick skillet, bring oil to medium high. Add cubed chicken and cook until light golden brown on all sides. Remove chicken and place on a paper towel. Drain oil and wipe out skillet with a paper towel.

Add chicken and OJ mixture to the skillet. Toss to coat chicken. Cook on medium heat until sauce has thickened, about 5-10 minutes.

Remove chicken and place on a platter. Serve with rice and a vegetable — broccoli goes well with this.

Note

The sauce is good over oven-cooked chicken meatballs, mini meat meatballs for an appetizer, or as a sauce for chicken wings.

Submitted by: Barbara McKinley, Centre Daily Times

Favorite thing about this recipe: Easy and the sauce makes it good.

Healthy Harvest Slow Cooker Chili

- 1 lb ground venison (or ground beef)
- 1 medium onion, chopped
- 1 large green pepper, chopped
- 1-2 jalapeño or poblano peppers, chopped
- 2 cloves garlic, minced
- 2 Tbsp chili powder
- 1 Tbsp paprika
- 1 Tbsp oregano
- 1/2 tsp ground black pepper
- 1/2 tsp cinnamon
- 4 drops stevia
- 1-2 tsp salt
- 1 can black beans, drained and rinsed
- 1 cup pumpkin or sweet potato, diced
- 14.5-oz can diced tomatoes
- 2 cups vegetable (or beef) broth

Total time: 8 hours, 30 minutes
Serves 8

In a skillet, brown the meat. Add onion, peppers, garlic and spices, and cook for a few minutes.

Dump into slow cooker. Add the rest of the ingredients, stir to combine. Cook on low 8 hours.

To thicken, if desired, mash some of the cooked beans and sweet potato. Taste for seasoning. Serve with shredded cheese, tortilla chips or cornbread.

Submitted by: Lisa Schneider, Centre Daily Times

Favorite thing about this recipe: It's healthy, easy and tastes even better the next day. I enjoy using my own garden produce for this recipe.

Chunky Roasted Vegetable Soup

- 3 cups water
- 1 cup red lentils
- 2 large parsnips, peeled and cut into chunks
- 2 large carrots, peeled and cut into chunks
- 2 celery stalks, cut into chunks
- 2 large onions, peeled and cut into chunks
- 10 baby potatoes, peeled and cut in halves or quarters
- 3 Tbsp olive oil
- Salt and pepper
- 3 cups vegetable or beef stock
- 2 cups packed fresh sliced mushrooms
- 3 cups packed coarsely chopped kale, thick stems removed
- 1 tsp thyme
- 1 tsp sage
- 1 tsp rosemary
- 1 cup cooked, drained, loose sweet Italian sausage (optional)
- 1/2 cup dry red wine
- 1/4 cup apple cider vinegar
- Olive oil, salt and pepper to taste

Total time: 1 hour
Serves 4-6

Heat oven to 350 F.

Combine water and lentils in a big stew pot, bring to a boil and simmer 30 minutes or until lentils begin to break down and dissolve.

In a large bowl, combine parsnips, carrots, celery, onions and potatoes and toss with oil, salt and pepper to coat. Spread on a lined sheet pan and roast in oven 30 minutes or until edges begin to brown, turning once after 15 minutes.

To pot with lentils, add stock, mushrooms, kale, herbs and cooked sausage (optional), bring to a boil, reduce to simmer and stir occasionally for 5 minutes or until kale begins to wilt. Fold in roasted vegetables and stir. Simmer until potato chunks are just fork-tender. Add wine and vinegar. Season to taste.

Ladle into large soup bowls and serve with crusty bread and cheese for a complete meal. For thinner texture, add more stock.

Submitted by: Anne Hoag, Centre Daily Times

Favorite thing about this recipe: Makes a vegan, gluten-free meal; or served with crusty bread and cheese, it's hearty fare.

Veggie Stuffed Shells

- 1 medium sweet potato
- 1 box jumbo pasta shells
- 2 tsp olive oil
- 1 cup zucchini, diced
- 1 cup mushroom, diced
- Salt and pepper
- 1 egg
- 1 cup ricotta
- 1/4 cup fresh parsley, chopped
- 1/4 cup Parmesan cheese, grated
- 1 cup shredded mozzarella
- 4 cups marinara sauce

Total time: 2 hours
Serves 6-8

Heat oven to 350.

Roast sweet potato in skin for about 45 minutes or until soft. Meanwhile, bring a large pot of salted water to a boil. Cook the pasta shells until al dente, drain and set aside.

In pan, heat oil to medium heat, until it shimmers, then add the zucchini and mushrooms. Season with salt and pepper. Cook about 5 minutes. Remove from heat and set aside.

Make filling: In large mixing bowl, crack egg and lightly beat. Add ricotta, parsley, Parmesan and 1/2 cup of the mozzarella. Squeeze cooked sweet potato from the skin and incorporate it into the filling. Add the diced, sauteed veggies.

Assemble dish: Spread 1-2 cups of marinara sauce on the bottom of 9x12 casserole dish. Fill each cooked pasta shell with 2 Tbsp of the filling and line up in rows on the dish, seam side up. Cover with remaining sauce and sprinkle with remaining mozzarella.

Cover with foil and bake 35 minutes. Uncover and bake another 10 minutes, until bubbly and browning.

Submitted by: Courtney Lyons, The Charlotte Observer

Favorite thing about this recipe: Delicious, lots of nutrients and easy to make in multiple batches to feed a crowd or freeze for another night.

Key Lime Marmalade Salmon

Salmon

- 2 lbs salmon, skin removed, cut in 4 equal pieces
- 1 lime, cut in half
- Salt and pepper to taste

Marinade

- 1/3 cup key lime marmalade (such as James Keiller & Son Dundee)
- 1/4 cup orange juice
- 2 Tbsp honey
- 1 Tbsp duck sauce
- 1 tsp hot mustard sauce

Total time: 30 minutes
Serves 4

Heat oven to 425 F.

Place salmon pieces in glass baking dish. Squeeze juice from 1/2 a lime over salmon. Salt and pepper to taste.

Make marinade: Whisk marmalade well. Add other ingredients and whisk all together. Pour all the marinade over salmon pieces. Let sit 10-15 minutes.

Transfer salmon to a foil-lined baking sheet. Bake 13-15 minutes.

Optional: Broil for an additional minute to "seal" marinade.

Before serving, squeeze lime juice from reserved 1/2 a lime over salmon *or* slice remaining lime and serve a slice next to each fillet.

Submitted by: Mindy Kirshbaum, The Charlotte Observer

Favorite thing about this recipe: Very attractive on a plate, and uses marmalade as a base!

Pan-Seared Trout with Field Peas

photo on page 86

- Olive oil
- 1/2 cup celery, chopped
- 1/4 cup onion, diced
- 1/2 cup fennel, chopped
- 1 cup field (or crowder) peas
- 2-2 1/2 cups chicken broth
- 2 N.C. Mountain Trout fillets (or available trout)
- 1 cup cherry tomatoes
- Salt and pepper
- Fresh Italian parsley, finely chopped for garnish

Total time: 1 hour, 15 minutes
Serves 2

In a saute pan with high sides, heat 2 Tbsp oil over medium-low heat. Add celery, onion and fennel, and saute until slightly softened and fragrant, about 5 minutes. Add peas, stirring, and broth. Season with salt and pepper and bring to a simmer. Simmer uncovered, stirring occasionally, until peas are tender. This may take 30-45 minutes.

Season trout with salt and pepper. In a separate pan, heat 1Tbsp oil over medium-high heat and saute trout for 3-5 minutes on the skin side then turn and cook another 1-2 minutes.

In a small pan, heat 1 tsp oil over medium-high heat. Add tomatoes and cook, stirring occasionally until blistered and fragrant. Season with salt and pepper.

To serve, season peas mixture to taste and divide evenly between 2 shallow bowls with cooking liquid. Place trout on top and top with blistered tomatoes. Garnish with parsley.

Submitted by: Sheryl Gerrard, The Charlotte Observer

Favorite thing about this recipe: Makes use of many local seasonal ingredients and things from our home garden.

The Best Lamb Chops

- 2 cloves garlic
- 1 tsp salt
- 3/4 cup lemon juice
- 6-8 lamb chops
- 1 tsp seven spice mix
- 3 cups cabbage, rough chopped
- 1 tomato

Total time: 6 hours, 10 minutes
Serves 3-4

Crush garlic with salt and lemon juice. Set aside.

In baking dish, put lamb chops in a single layer. Poke holes in lamb chops with a fork. Turn chops over and poke holes in second side. Sprinkle seven spices mix on chops and turn over and sprinkle on other side. Pour garlic/salt/lemon juice over chops. Cover and place in refrigerator for several hours or overnight.

After several hours turn chops over.

In the morning, put cabbage in slow cooker to cover the bottom. Lay chops on top of cabbage. Pour marinade over chops. Slice tomato and place one slice on top of each chop. Sprinkle tomato with a little salt and a little seven spice. Cook in slow cooker on high for 5 or 6 hours, or on low for 6 or 7 hours. Each slow cooker can vary so keep an eye on it.

Submitted by: Jean Khalil, The State

Favorite thing about this recipe: It cooks in a slow cooker!

Jerry's World Famous Chili

- Olive oil
- 1 lb lean ground beef
- 2 small cans V-8 Juice
- 1 can RO*TEL Mild Diced Tomatoes and Green Chilies
- 1 can Italian stewed tomatoes
- 1 Vidalia onion, chopped
- 1 tsp cumin
- 1 tsp chili powder
- Tabasco sauce

Total time: 3 hours
Serves 4

In a large pot, cover bottom with olive oil and heat for a few minutes. Add 1 lb lean ground beef and cook until browned. Add V-8 Juice, diced tomatoes, stewed tomatoes, onion, season with spices and Tabasco sauce. Cook over medium heat for 2 hours.

Submitted by: Jerry Clem, The State

Favorite thing about this recipe: The taste!

Texas Barbecued Pot Roast

- 4 lb pot roast
- 2 Tbsp vegetable oil
- 1 1/2 cups onions, sliced
- 1 large clove garlic, minced
- 2 tsp salt
- 1/2 tsp freshly ground pepper
- 8-oz can tomato sauce
- 1/4 cup chili sauce
- 1/2 cup cider vinegar
- 2 Tbsp brown sugar
- 2 tsp Worcestershire sauce
- 1/2 cup water
- 2 tsp chili powder

Total time: 2 hours, 45 minutes
Serves 8

Trim fat from meat. In a Dutch oven or a heavy skillet, heat oil and brown meat on all sides. Add onions and garlic and cook until browned. Mix in salt, pepper and tomato sauce. Cover and cook over low heat for 1 1/2 hours.

In a bowl, combine the chili sauce, vinegar, sugar, Worcestershire sauce, water and chili powder and stir in to skillet with meat. Cover again and cook at least 1 hour longer or until tender. Skim fat from gravy. The gravy is wonderful on mashed potatoes.

Submitted by: Charlie Dill, The Herald-Sun

Favorite thing about this recipe: It tastes great!!!!

Pan-Seared Salmon with Sauteed Mushrooms and Dirty Rice

photo on page 81

- 1 tsp kosher salt, divided
- 1 tsp ground black pepper, divided
- 2 tsp garlic powder, divided
- 1 tsp frozen orange juice
- 3 Tbsp white wine
- 3 Tbsp, plus 1/2 cup olive oil
- 1 1/2 lb salmon fillet
- 1/2 cup breadcrumbs
- 8 oz mushrooms (white button, baby bella or cremini)
- 1 Tbsp sherry vinegar
- 1 cup rice, cooked

Total time: 1 hour, 30 minutes
Serves 4

A Note About Salmon

Use wild-caught Pacific, fresh or previously frozen fillets, sliced crosswise as small steaks. Do not use farm-raised Atlantic salmon!

In a bowl, combine 1/2 tsp kosher salt, 1/2 tsp ground pepper, 1 tsp garlic powder, frozen OJ, white wine and 3 Tbsp olive oil.

Place salmon in glass baking dish and pour marinade over. Leave for 45 minutes. Tip: in a pinch you can use Italian Zesty salad dressing; do not use anything spicy, such as barbecue or jerk sauce.

Coat marinating salmon with breadcrumbs.

While salmon is marinating, prep mushrooms — wipe down with moist paper towel (do not rinse) and slice.

In a large nonstick shallow fry pan, add a thin layer of olive oil and heat to medium. Add marinated and breaded salmon. Cook until done to your liking — about 5 minutes on each side, with nice golden color — place on a serving dish.

Remove about 1/2 the oil in the pan and save it.

To the pan with remaining oil, add mushrooms, cook on both sides until golden brown. Add 1/2 tsp salt, 1/2 tsp pepper, 1 tsp garlic powder and sherry vinegar, swirl around and place on a serving dish.

Pour back the saved oil on the same pan, add cooked rice — mix rice up with the "dirty" oil with flecks of salmon and mushrooms pieces left on the pan, then place on a serving dish.

Now you have a one-pan, complete three-item meal — protein, fiber and carb! Enjoy with a glass of white wine!

Submitted by: Mrinmay Biswas, The Herald-Sun

Favorite thing about this recipe: I use salmon that I catch in Alaska!

Great Grandma's Ham Fluff

- 2 cups milk
- 1 Tbsp butter
- Paprika
- 1/3 cup cornmeal
- 1 cup grated cheese
- 3 egg yolks (egg whites saved)
- 1 cup ground ham

Total time: 15 minutes
Serves 3-4

Heat oven to 350 F.

In saucepan, heat milk to boiling point, add the butter and dash of paprika. Slowly stir in cornmeal, and boil 5 minutes. Stir in grated cheese. Cook slowly until cheese is melted and remove from heat. Beat egg yolks and stir into mixture along with ground ham. Whip egg whites to stiff peaks and fold into mixture. Bake in well-greased 8x8 dish for 40 minutes.

Submitted by: Martha Ruddy, The Fresno Bee

Favorite thing about this recipe: Fluffy and flavorful.

Basil Sausage Bruschetta a la Mozzarella

- 4 Italian sausages (hot, mild or sweet), cut into bite-size pieces
- Olive oil
- 1 loaf Italian bread, sliced in half lengthwise
- 2 Tbsp basil paste
- 1 clove garlic, crushed (or 1 Tbsp garlic spread)
- 2 Campari tomatoes, sliced
- Dried oregano
- 5 slices fresh Mozzarella cheese (per cut loaf)
- Parmesan cheese (optional)

Total time: 25 minutes
Serves 4

Heat oven to 350 F.

In pan, cook sausage to almost perfection in your favorite oil. On baking sheet, arrange Italian bread with cut sides up. Spread basil paste on the bread first, then add crushed garlic or garlic spread. Next, add sliced tomatoes and the cooked sausage. Sprinkle a dash or two of oregano and the sliced mozzarella, drizzle with olive oil. Place in oven for 10 minutes or until mozzarella is melted. Can add a sprinkle of Parmesan cheese.

Submitted by: Gina Meyers, The Fresno Bee

Favorite thing about this recipe: Easy and tasty.

J's Slow Cooker Lasagna

photo on page 82

- 1 lb ground turkey (or meat of choice)
- Salt
- Pepper
- Garlic powder
- 1/2 onion, chopped
- Uncooked lasagna noodles
- 2 jars Ragu Old World Style Traditional sauce (or marinara sauce of choice)
- 4 oz shredded mozzarella cheese
- One 15-oz part-skim ricotta cheese
- 1 cup Parmesan cheese, grated

Total time: 5 hours, 15 minutes
Serves 6-10

Season ground meat with salt, pepper and garlic powder to taste and cook in frying pan. Add chopped onion to ground meat and cook until onions are tender.

Add both jars of sauce; stir and remove from heat and set aside.

In a bowl, combine ricotta, mozzarella and Parmesan cheeses, and stir until mixed evenly.

In slow cooker, add 1/4 of sauce mixture to cover bottom. Add one layer of lasagna noodles. Spread cheese mixture over noodles. Spread sauce mixture over cheese. Add another layer of noodles, cheese and sauce mixture. Add one last layer of noodles across top and cover any leftover sauce.

Cover and cook on high for 4-5 hours.

Submitted by: Jenelle Hamblin, The News Tribune (Tacoma)

Favorite thing about this recipe: Simple, easy and the BEST tasting lasagna that the whole family will love! I have given this recipe out and everyone has said it was a game changer and family loved it, including kiddos.

Chicken Cacciatore

photo on page 83

- 2 Tbsp olive oil
- 1/2 cup white onion, chopped
- 1/2 cup green bell pepper, chopped
- 2 carrots, chopped
- 2 celery stalks, chopped
- 1/2 acorn squash, skin on, cubed
- 1/2 cup white wine
- 24-oz jar marinara sauce
- 1 tsp Italian spice blend
- 1 lb chicken thighs, deboned and skin removed, cubed
- Fresh basil leaves
- Parmesan cheese
- Pasta of your choice

Total time: 1 hour
Serves 4

Heat oven to 275 F.

In an oven safe Dutch oven, add 1 Tbsp of olive oil and saute the onion for 3 minutes. Add the bell pepper, carrots and celery, saute for another 3 minutes. Add the acorn squash and the wine with vegetables to deglaze the pot. Add the marinara sauce and Italian spices.

In a nonstick skillet, add 1 Tbsp of olive oil and brown the chicken pieces on all sides. *Do not cook chicken all the way through.* Add the chicken pieces to the Dutch oven with vegetables.

Cover the pot and place in the oven for 2 hours.

Serve with fresh chopped basil and a sprinkle of Parmesan cheese over your favorite pasta. Enjoy!

Submitted by: Hilda Vandergriff, The Fresno Bee

Favorite thing about this recipe: The taste and smell.

Breakfast Tostada

- 1/3 cup cabbage
- 1 onion, sliced
- 1 bell pepper (optional)
- Red pepper flakes
- Salt
- Pepper
- Apple cider vinegar
- Refried beans, warmed
- 3 scrambled eggs
- Corn tortillas, heated
- Toppings: chopped tomatoes, avocado, cilantro and your favorite salsa

Total time: 30 minutes
Serves 2

In pan, stir fry cabbage, onion and bell peppers (if using), season with red pepper flakes, salt and pepper to taste. Once vegetables are cooked, remove from heat and drizzle with apple cider vinegar.

Stack refried beans, eggs, cooked veggies on corn tortillas in order listed above. Add toppings.

Submitted by: Elizabeth Braden, The Fresno Bee

Favorite thing about this recipe: You eat with your eyes first and it is beautiful, colorful, appetizing and delicious!!

Pecan-Encrusted Chicken Breast

- 2/3 cup chopped pecans
- 1/3 cup Parmesan cheese, grated
- 1 chicken breast, pounded flat
- 2 Tbsp butter

Sauce

- 1 cup apricot preserves
- 1 Tbsp minced garlic
- 1 tsp Teriyaki sauce

Total time: 30 minutes
Serves 2

Blend the pecans and Parmesan and coat chicken breast completely.

Melt butter in a saute pan, and cook the chicken 20 minutes, turning midway. Cover with a lid and lower heat to cook chicken thoroughly while making sure not to burn the nut mixture. Place cooked chicken on plate when done. Note: Breast size determines time to cook.

In a saucepan, blend all the sauce ingredients and cook in until garlic is done, about 5 minutes. Pour over the chicken breast and serve.

Submitted by: Deborah Scott, The Fresno Bee

Favorite thing about this recipe: Easy and delicious flavor.

Tater Tot-Topped Chicken Pot Pie

photo on page 84

- 1 Tbsp extra-virgin olive oil
- 1/4 medium onion, chopped
- 1 medium carrot, chopped
- 1/2 large celery stalk, chopped
- 1 tsp kosher salt
- 1 tsp ground black pepper
- 2 tsp garlic powder or 2 cloves garlic, diced
- 1 Tbsp dried thyme or 2 Tbsp fresh thyme leaves, chopped
- 1 1/2 Tbsp cornstarch (flour can be substituted)
- 1 1/4 cups chicken broth
- 1 1/4 cups (about 8 oz) cooked chicken breast, diced
- 3/4 cup frozen peas
- 44 mini or 24 regular size, frozen tater tots

Total time: 50 minutes
Serves 2

Heat oven to 350 F.

In a large, high-sided, oven-safe skillet, heat oil over a medium heat, add vegetables and spices. Cook until vegetables are soft, about 4 minutes.

Whisk the cornstarch into the chicken broth. Pour the chicken broth/cornstarch mixture the into the skillet, bring to a simmer. Cook about 5 minutes more, until slightly thickened. Stir in the chicken and peas and simmer 2 minutes more.

If you are going to use individual serving bowls, scoop 1/2 the pot pie mixture into each. Whether you use two bowls or the one skillet, arrange the frozen tater tots in a circular pattern over the mixture.

Bake until the tater tots are golden brown, 35-40 minutes. Check at 35 minutes.

Submitted by: Stephen Mettee, The Fresno Bee

Favorite thing about this recipe: Delicious and filling but only about 400 calories.

Squeaky Pork and Beans

photo on page 90

- 1-2 Tbsp oil
- 1 onion, chopped
- 1/4-1/2 tsp red pepper flakes
- 1 lb ground pork (or any ground meat to your liking)
- 2 tsp garlic, minced
- 1 bunch Asian longbeans or 1 1/2 lbs green beans, cut in 2-inch pieces
- 1/2 cup oyster sauce
- 1-2 Tbsp sambal oelek (Indonesian chili paste)
- 1 can sliced water chestnuts, drained and rinsed
- 1-2 cups fresh bean sprouts, rinsed
- Steamed rice of your choosing

Total time: 45 minutes
Serves 4-5

In a large skillet, heat oil or wok over medium-high heat. Add the onion, toss and fry for 3-4 minutes. If using, add the red pepper flakes and stir.

Add the ground pork and garlic, stirring until the meat is no longer pink. To the meat mixture, toss in the beans and continue to stir fry all the ingredients together.

Add the oyster sauce and the sambal oelek. Once the sauces are mixed in, add the water chestnuts. When the beans are cooked to the desired liking, add in the bean sprouts, stirring everything together.

Take off the heat and serve over steamed rice.

Submitted by: Julie Laird, The Fresno Bee

Favorite thing about this recipe: The textures and the flavor!

Pounded Chicken

- 4 skinless boneless chicken breasts
- 3/4 cup flour
- 2 eggs
- 1 1/2 cups garlic and herb breadcrumbs
- 1/2 cup butter
- 10.5-oz can cream of mushroom with roasted garlic soup
- 8 oz baby bella mushrooms
- 1 cup Marsala cooking wine

Total time: 50 minutes
Serves 4

Prepare chicken breasts: Rinse chicken and pat dry with paper towels. Cut away the visible fat. Then place chicken one at a time in a big zip-close bag and pound both sides with a mallet. You want the chicken to be about 1/2-inch thick.

Next get out three separate bowls. We will use these to dip the chicken into to batter it. In the first bowl, place flour. In second bowl, crack two eggs and gently beat. In the third bowl, place garlic and herb breadcrumbs.

Place pounded chicken in flour first, then flip and coat in flour, then in the egg, and lastly the breadcrumbs. Then place battered chicken on a plate for now. Coat all four chicken breasts.

In a large skillet, add 4 Tbsp butter, let melt and cook chicken on medium heat, browning chicken on both sides, flipping the chicken occasionally. If you cannot fit all four pieces of chicken in one batch then do them in two separate batches just to brown them. Set browned chicken aside on a plate.

To pan, add the other 4 Tbsp butter, still on medium heat, and add the mushrooms. Let the mushrooms cook about 10 minutes until they are brown, stirring occasionally. Place mushrooms in a bowl, set aside.

Lower heat to simmer. To skillet, add cream of mushroom soup. Add Marsala cooking wine. Turn heat to high, whisk until smooth. Reduce heat to simmer, add in chicken and mushrooms. Cover the skillet and let simmer for 30 minutes. Chicken should be at 165 F.

Submitted by: Rebecca Nichols, The Fresno Bee

Favorite thing about this recipe: "Pounded Chicken" was one of my favorite dishes and a family classic. My mother called it that probably because you could hear her preparing the dish as in "pounding the chicken" from every room in the house! She passed it along to me and it's very tasty!

Chili Cheese Dog Tater Tot Casserole

- 1 package hot dog buns
- 1 package hot dogs
- 2 cups tater tots
- 1 can chili
- Cheese (8 slices or 2 cups shredded)

Total time: 45 minutes
Serves 4-6

Heat oven to 375 F.

In a casserole dish, layer buns, hot dogs, tots, chili and cheese — there should be two layers of each. You can either cut up the bread and hot dogs, or leave them whole. Bake for 30 minutes.

Submitted by: Kaye Sheets, Fort Worth Star-Telegram

Favorite thing about this recipe: It's easy and always good, very hard to mess up, and you can switch out cheeses or leave out tots or hot dogs, if so inclined.

Peanut Butter Banana Sandwich

- 2 bananas
- 8 slices bread (Texas toast)
- 1 jar peanut butter, creamy or crunchy
- 1/2 cup margarine or butter

Total time: 20 minutes
Serves 4

Heat oven to 350 F.

Mash bananas in bowl until it looks like spread. Spread banana on one slice of bread, peanut butter on the other. Sandwich together, place on buttered cooking sheet or butter the sandwiches for flipping to brown in oven.

Cook 7 minutes on one side, 3 the other. Take out, then enjoy with honey, ice cream, french fries, onion rings or hot cocoa (my personal favorite is soup).

Submitted by: Lasondra Huggins, Fort Worth Star-Telegram

Favorite thing about this recipe: Tastes great and filling.

Greg's King Ranch Pot Pie Casserole

photo on page 88

- 2 cups frozen vegetables
- 1 cup frozen pepper/onions
- 5 cloves freshly minced garlic
- 1 can RO*TEL
- 1 can mushroom soup
- 1 can chicken broth
- Salt
- Pepper
- 1 squirt Sriracha sauce
- 3 cups leftover Chicken Express strips (or chicken tenders), chopped
- Leftover Mexican Inn chips (or Fritos style chips), broken up
- 4 slices American cheese
- 2 cups cheddar cheese

Total time: 45 minutes
Serves 4-6

Heat oven to 350 F.

In large covered, oven-safe roasting pan, saute all frozen veggies. Add minced garlic and saute. Add all cans and spices/Sriracha in and mix well. Add chicken, chips, sliced cheese. Mix well and flatten down.

Bake covered for 25 minutes. Remove lid and top with shredded cheese. Bake another 15 minutes. Eat.

Submitted by: Cecil Harper, Fort Worth Star-Telegram

Favorite thing about this recipe: It's good.

Supreme Bean Nachos

- 1 lb ground beef
- 1 can refried beans
- 7 oz cheese sauce
- 9 oz sour cream
- 1/2 bag of tortilla chips

Total time: 15 minutes
Serves 3-5

In a medium-size skillet, cook the ground beef about 5-10 minutes on high or until browned.

In a medium or large mixing bowl (that's microwave safe), mix refried beans, cheese sauce and sour cream together. Heat the mixture in the microwave for about 2-7 minutes on medium or high power until warm.

Then add the ground beef to the bean mixture and stir the meat in well.

Pour tortilla chips on a plate and put the toppings on that and enjoy your Supreme Bean Nachos.

Submitted by: Aaron Hahn, Fort Worth Star-Telegram

Favorite thing about this recipe: My favorite part about it is when I make my bean cream and then add the cheese and ground beef to make delicious nachos!

Leftover Turkey Cuban Sandwich

- Sub roll bread
- Leftover Thanksgiving turkey
- Shaved ham
- Sliced pickles
- Sliced horseradish cheese
- Spicy mayo dipping sauce

Caramelized Onions

- Sliced onion
- Olive oil
- Sugar
- Salt and pepper

Total time: 15 minutes
Serves 2

Caramelize onions prepared with olive oil, sugar, salt and pepper.

Brush bread with mayo. Build up Cuban-style sandwich by placing leftover turkey, ham, caramelized onions, cheese and pickles. Use panini press and reserve extra spicy mayo for dipping sauce.

Submitted by: Murray Yanker, The Island Packet

Favorite thing about this recipe: The caramelized onions.

Beef Cacciatore

photo on page 81

- 1/4 cup olive oil
- Medium onion, chopped
- 1/4 cup flour
- 1 tsp salt
- 1/4 tsp pepper
- 1 tsp Italian seasoning
- 3 lbs beef chuck, cut into 1-inch cubes
- 2 cloves garlic, minced
- 1 bay leaf
- 1/2 tsp dried crushed red pepper
- 14-oz can beef broth
- 1/2 cup red wine
- 2-lb can whole tomatoes
- 2 large green peppers, cut into 1-inch squares

Total time: 2 hours
Serves 8-10

In heavy skillet, cover bottom with oil. Brown the onions and remove to a separate dish.

Put flour, salt, pepper and Italian seasoning into a paper bag and put the meat in. Shake well. Brown the meat in oil a few pieces at a time to ensure good browning.

Crush garlic in salt and add to the meat with onions, bay leaf and red pepper. Pour about 1/2 of the broth over the meat and simmer for 1 1/2-2 hours. Check it occasionally and add more broth if necessary.

Add wine and let steep, covered, for 3 minutes.

Add tomatoes and simmer for another 15 minutes.

Add peppers and cook 10 more minutes.

Add reserved flour to some broth and stir into gravy to thicken.

Serve over fettuccine or wide noodles.

Submitted by: Shirley Potter, Fort Worth Star-Telegram

Favorite thing about this recipe: Everybody loves Italian.

California Pilaf

- 1 lb ground beef
- 4.5-oz can ripe olives, chopped
- 1/3 cup green peppers, chopped
- 1/3 cup onion, chopped
- 1/2 tsp garlic power
- 1/2 cup uncooked rice
- 2 cups hot water
- 6-oz can tomato paste
- 1/2 tsp salt
- 1/4 tsp pepper
- 1 Tbsp steak sauce
- 1 Tbsp Worcestershire sauce

Total time: 1 hour, 30 minutes
Serves 3-4

Heat oven 350 F.
　Brown the meat.
　Combine meat with all other ingredients in a casserole dish.
　Bake for 1 hour.

Submitted by: Margaret Gagliardi, Fort Worth Star-Telegram

Favorite thing about this recipe: Fast, delicious and easy.

Sweet and Savory Marinated Steak

- 1 cup low-sodium soy sauce
- 1 Tbsp sugar
- 1/4 tsp oregano
- 1/2 tsp dry mustard
- 1/8 tsp garlic powder
- 1/2 tsp ground ginger
- 1/8 tsp tarragon
- 1/8 tsp marjoram
- 2 Tbsp whiskey
- 2 lb flank steak

Total time: 5 hours, 25 minutes
Serves 6

In a medium size mixing bowl, combine all ingredients for the marinade and whisk thoroughly.
　Pour over the meat, cover and place in the refrigerator for 5 hours or longer.
　Heat grill to 425 F. Cook steak until preferred doneness: 3-4 minutes per side. Rest for 10 minutes.
　Slice across the grain and serve.

Submitted by: Travis Kincade, Fort Worth Star-Telegram

Favorite thing about this recipe: It's the perfect combination of sweet and savory on a great cut of beef that is often overlooked.

Nanny's Cornbread Dressing

- 3 1/2 lbs cooked cornbread
- 6 cooked biscuits (can use canned biscuits)
- 1 cup celery, chopped
- 1 cup onion, chopped
- 1 cup vegetable oil
- 2-3 tsp ground sage
- 6 packets Herb-Ox chicken bouillon (found in broth section)
- 4 eggs
- 2 quarts chicken broth
- Salt and pepper to taste
- Cooking spray

Giblet Gravy

- Cooked giblet from turkey or chicken
- 2 cans cream of chicken soup
- 1-2 cans broth, depending on the thickness you like
- 3 boiled eggs, chopped
- Salt and pepper to taste
- 1 packet Herb-Ox chicken bouillon

Total time: 2 hours
Serves 12

Heat oven to 350 F.

In a large bowl, crumble cooked cornbread and biscuits. Add all ingredients, but add broth slowly at the last.

Preferably with your hands (be sure they are sanitized), mix all ingredients. It should use close to the 2 quarts of broth. The mixture should be "mushy."

Spray a large baking dish with cooking spray. Pour in mixture and bake for approximately 45 minutes. It should be bubbling on the sides and fairly firm. If you like firmer dressing, cook a little longer but the taste is better if it is not dry.

Make giblet gravy: Stir all ingredients and heat.

YUM!

Submitted by: Tjwanah Smith, Fort Worth Star-Telegram

Favorite thing about this recipe: My mother (Nanny) was famous for this dressing. I now use it in my catering business. Plus, it is delectable.

Margarita Salmon

photo on page 88

- 2 1/2 lbs salmon fillet, skinned and boned
- 4 limes, plus more for serving
- 2 Tbsp kosher salt
- 2 Tbsp coarse ground black pepper
- 2 Tbsp lemon pepper
- 1/2 cup fresh cilantro, rough chopped
- Cooking spray, as needed

Total time: 40 minutes
Serves 6

Heat oven to 350 F.

Trim and discard the very thin portion of the "belly." If you want, cut out the dark "blood line" running the length of the salmon (it often has a very fishy taste). Cut the salmon into 6 equal fillets.

Using a microplane grater, grate the rind from three of the limes to make fine zest. Cut the zested limes in half and squeeze the juice over the salmon. Using a sharp paring knife, cut thin zest strips from the fourth lime and reserve. Cut the fourth lime into four wedges.

In a shallow bowl, mix salt, pepper and lemon pepper. Stir in the zest and cilantro and mix well.

Spray the cut side of the salmon lightly with the cooking spray and dip the sprayed side into the salt/herb mixture evenly coating each fillet.

Lightly spray a nonstick or well-seasoned pan with spray and set it over medium-high heat. Place salmon, seasoned side down, in the hot pan. Cook fillets about 2 minutes or nicely browned. Turn over taking care to keep the crust intact. Brown second side for about 2 minutes.

Place salmon fillets on baking pan and garnish with lime zest strips before placing salmon in the oven for about 5 minutes to finish cooking.

Salmon should be firm to the touch and flake nicely with a fork. Serve with the lime wedges.

Submitted by: Bob Rosar, Fort Worth Star-Telegram

Favorite thing about this recipe: Salmon is becoming more and more affordable. This is great news considering its health benefits, ease of preparation and great taste. This is one of my family's favorites and one of my most requested entrees. Leftovers are great cold on a salad.

Seared Flat Iron Steak with Horseradish Cream

photo on page 82

Steak

- 2 Tbsp garlic, minced
- 2 Tbsp olive oil
- 3/4 tsp kosher salt
- 1 tsp coarse ground black pepper
- 1/2 tsp fresh thyme, minced
- 3/4-2 lbs flat iron steak, single piece

Horseradish Cream

- 1/2 cup sour cream
- 3 Tbsp prepared horseradish, jarred
- 3 Tbsp mayonnaise
- 1/4 tsp kosher salt
- 1/8 tsp coarse ground black pepper
- 1 tsp chives, freeze-dried

Total time: 3 hours, 25 minutes
Serves 4

Steak

Place all the ingredients except the steak in a large resealable bag. Seal the bag and mix the ingredients together. Open the bag and add the steak. Press out as much air as you can and seal the bag. Marinate in the refrigerator for at least 3 hours or overnight.

Remove the steak from the marinade and pat dry. Discard the marinade.

Heat a skillet (cast-iron works best) or a grill pan over medium-high heat. Sear the steak in the hot skillet for 3-4 minutes on each side for medium rare (or more or less to your preference of doneness). Allow steak to rest for about 3 minutes before serving.

Be sure to cut against the grain, which on a flat iron steak is slicing on the thinner side.

For an added treat, throw some cherry or grape tomatoes in the pan when cooking the steak and allow to slightly char.

Horseradish Cream

Combine all ingredients. Keep refrigerated and serve chilled. Can be made the day before.

Submitted by: Bob Rosar, Fort Worth Star-Telegram

Favorite thing about this recipe: Flat iron steak is an often overlooked cut of beef. Flavorful with a little chew, but not tough. When sliced the right way it becomes tender. There is minimum fat and no sinew or gristle. A fan favorite on the grill.

Layered Tex-Mex-Pasta

- 1 lb ground beef or Italian sausage
- 1/2 onion, chopped
- 1 clove garlic, chopped
- Black pepper
- Garlic powder
- Lawry's Seasoned Salt
- Chili powder
- 1 can refried beans or black beans
- 1 package small elbow macaroni or shell pasta
- 1 jar spaghetti sauce
- 2-4 cups of mozzarella, cheddar and Monterey Jack cheeses mixed together
- Garnishes (optional): black olives, sour cream and/or salsa

Total time: 1 hour
Serves 4-6

Heat oven to 350 F.

In a skillet, brown ground beef or Italian sausage. Add chopped onion, garlic and seasonings to taste.

While the meat is cooking, open the can of refried beans or black beans. Spray a casserole pan or dish with cooking spray and then spread the beans on the bottom of the pan or dish.

Drain meat from the skillet and then add the jar of spaghetti sauce to the meat, let simmer on low heat.

Next, bring a pot of water to boil then add the package of pasta of your choice to the boiling water until tender.

Layer the meat sauce over the beans, followed by a layer of pasta over the meat sauce and sprinkle your blended cheeses over the pasta.

Repeat layers until you reach the top of the pan or dish with the blended cheeses ending on top.

Place the Layered Tex-Mex-Pasta in oven for 40 minutes. Remove from oven and serve with suggested toppings.

Submitted by: Trina Sanders, Fort Worth Star-Telegram

Favorite thing about this recipe: Layered flavors.

Diana's Lasagna

- 1 box lasagna noodles
- 8-oz package shredded cheddar cheese
- 8-oz package shredded or sliced Swiss cheese (slices cut up)
- 8-oz package shredded mozzarella cheese
- 8-oz package muenster cheese, cut up
- 1 large jar Ragu sauce
- 1 small can tomato paste
- 2 cans tomato sauce
- 1 lb hamburger, cooked and shredded
- 2 Tbsp oregano, divided
- 1 Tbsp garlic powder
- 1 egg

Total time: 45 minutes
Serves 6-8

Heat oven to 350 F.

Prepare the meat sauce by browning the hamburger, then add the Ragu sauce, tomato paste, tomato sauce, 1 Tbsp oregano and Italian seasoning to taste.

Mix the cheese, egg, 1 Tbsp oregano and garlic powder in a large bowl.

Cook lasagna noodles.

To assemble, alternate the 3 main ingredients: put some sauce around the bottom of a long pan, then noodles, hamburger sauce, then cheese. Repeat (You can double the recipe if necessary). Cover with foil and bake for about 30 minutes.

Submitted by: Diana Gouyton, Fort Worth Star-Telegram

Favorite thing about this recipe: It tastes so good and cheesy. A favorite with all my friends.

Magic German Apple Pancakes

photo on page 87

- 1/4 cup vegetable oil, plus 1 Tbsp additional for pans
- 2 cups all-purpose flour
- 4 Tbsp sugar, divided
- 1/2 tsp salt
- 1 Tbsp baking powder
- 1 3/4 cups milk (can use plant-based)
- 1 egg
- 1 medium Granny Smith apple, sliced 1/4-inch thick
- 1 tsp cinnamon

Total time: 40 minutes
Serves 4-6

Heat oven to 425 F.

In two cast-iron skillets, add 2 Tbsp oil to each to coat bottom.

In a large bowl, combine flour, 2 Tbsp sugar, salt and baking powder. Whisk to combine and set aside.

Combine milk, oil and egg; mix together. Add liquids to dry mix and whisk together.

Pour 1/2 of batter — dividing into bottom of both skillets. Add apple slices in circular pattern on top of batter in pans.

Sprinkle 1 Tbsp sugar and 1/2 tsp cinnamon on top of apples. Reserve remaining sugar and cinnamon for top.

Pour remaining batter over apples — dividing between both skillets.

Sprinkle remaining 1 Tbsp sugar and 1/2 tsp cinnamon to top layer of batter.

Bake 25 minutes or until brown.

Cut into wedges and serve.

Submitted by: Rosemarie Bray, Fort Worth Star-Telegram

Favorite thing about this recipe: My dad created this recipe back in the '80s. He's since passed away and I think of him and make these often in his memory.

Clean, Green Chili (Vegan)

- 1 Tbsp olive oil (for sauteing)
- 1 Tbsp garlic, chopped
- 1 small Vidalia onion, coarsely chopped
- 1 green pepper, coarsely chopped
- 1 red pepper, coarsely chopped
- 1 yellow pepper, coarsely chopped
- 1-2 packages plant-based crumbles or "meat"
- 1 cup each black beans, navy beans and kidney beans, canned or fresh
- 2 cups diced tomatoes, canned or fresh
- 1 can diced green chilies (or 1/4 cup fresh)
- 1 cup fire-roasted corn, canned or fresh
- 1 tsp cilantro
- 1 Tbsp prepared chili seasoning (or salt, pepper, red pepper, ground cumin)
- 1 Tbsp Better Than Bouillon Vegetable Base (follow directions on jar to prepare)
- 4-oz can black olives (or 1/2 cup fresh, sliced)

Total time: 2 hours
Serves 4-6

In a large stockpot (6-8 quarts), saute the garlic, onions and peppers until just soft, about 5 minutes.

Add crumbles and saute another 2 minutes, stirring frequently.

Drain beans and add to sauteed mixture, stir.

Add diced tomatoes (do not drain), stir.

Add all other ingredients except olives, bouillon and seasonings.

Stir the chili thoroughly before seasoning.

Add the seasonings and prepared bouillon, stir thoroughly.

Bring your chili to a boil, then immediately lower to a slow simmer.

After 45 minutes simmering stir in the olives. Simmer an additional 15 minutes.

Notes

Chili is a very personal concoction. Adjust seasonings to your taste.

Want more beans, crumbles or vegetables...add them.

You can add 1 hot pepper (jalapeño, ghost, Sriracha) to make the chili 3-alarm if desired.

You're a carnivore? Substitute 85% lean ground beef for plant-based.

Need an additional kick? Add plant-based sausage crumbles.

Want a smoky flavor? Add 1/4 tsp liquid smoke.

Submitted by: Deborah Colella, The Island Packet

Favorite thing about this recipe: It's low-fat and very adaptable to individual tastes.

Pollo e Pasta a la Vodka

- Olive oil
- 1 cup onions, chopped
- 2 cloves garlic, chopped
- 2 Tbsp parsley
- 1 tsp salt
- 2 tsp black pepper
- 2 tsp red pepper flakes
- 24-oz jar vodka sauce
- 2/3 cup milk
- 2 Tbsp vanilla yogurt
- 1 lb cooked chicken, chopped
- 1 lb cooked pasta (rotini or penne)

Total time: 1 hour
Serves 6

In a 6-quart pot, heat olive oil (enough to coat bottom) until hot. Saute onions until translucent; add garlic, parsley, salt, black pepper and red pepper flakes. Stir until garlic is cooked (only a few minutes) — watching closely so the garlic doesn't burn.

Add vodka sauce to the pot, stirring well. Pour the milk into the vodka jar and shake vigorously to extract all the sauce; add the yogurt to the pot, stirring well.

Simmer on low for 30 minutes, stirring frequently so the bottom of pot doesn't burn.

In a large pot, boil 6 quarts of water; add a bit of salt. Cook pasta according to directions on the box. Drain pasta well after cooking.

To serve, place sauce on bottom of the pasta dish; then add the pasta to the bowl. Top with more sauce and enjoy.

Notes

I use leftover rotisserie chicken for this meal minus the skin and bones. If necessary, I freeze leftovers until I have enough to make this meal.

I also make the enhanced vodka sauce in the morning allowing it to cool before I refrigerate it for dinner later in the day.

Submitted by: Diane Tucker, The Island Packet

Favorite thing about this recipe: Super easy and delicious.

Six Boy Taco

photo on page 92

- 1 small onion, chopped
- 1 lb ground beef
- 14.5-oz can diced tomatoes
- 1 tsp chili powder
- 1/2 tsp cumin
- 1/2 tsp oregano
- 1/2 tsp salt
- 1/2 cup rice, uncooked
- 1 can water (use tomato can)
- 1 bag original Fritos corn chips

Toppings

- Chopped green onion
- Shredded lettuce
- Grated cheddar cheese
- Chopped tomatoes
- Chopped avocado
- Sour cream
- Sliced olives
- Cilantro
- Favorite hot sauce

Total time: 45 minutes
Serves 4-6

In skillet, brown the onion and ground beef.

Add canned tomatoes, spices, rice and water. Cover and simmer for 20-25 minutes.

Meanwhile, prepare the rest of the toppings and present in individual bowls.

To serve, each person puts Fritos in their bowl, scoop some meat mixture on top and then add the various toppings you like.

Submitted by: Carol McBride, The Island Packet

Favorite thing about this recipe: Easy prep and cook. Beautiful taco bowls. Everyone can choose the things they like!

Indian Stew

- 1 lb hamburger meat
- 1/2 onion, chopped
- 1 clove garlic, grated
- 1/2 cup beef broth
- 1/2 tsp salt and pepper
- 1/2 tsp chili pepper
- 1 can ranch-style beans, drained
- 1 can kernel corn, drained
- 1 can stewed tomatoes
- 1 package cornbread mix
- Grated cheese (optional)

Total time: 25 minutes
Serves 8

Brown hamburger meat. Drain grease. Saute onion. Add grated garlic, beef broth, stir. Add salt, pepper and chili pepper. Stir in beans, corn and tomatoes. Heat.

Mix cornbread as package directs. Bake. Cut into large chunks.

Pour stew into bowls. Add cheese and cornbread on top.

Submitted by: Kelley Cates, Fort Worth Star-Telegram

Favorite thing about this recipe: Good on cool day.

Chicken Monterey

- 4 boneless, skinless chicken breasts
- 4 whole green chiles, canned
- 4 slices Jack cheese
- 4 Tbsp vegetable oil
- 1/2 cup breadcrumbs
- 1/4 cup Parmesan cheese, grated
- Up to 3 tsp chili powder, depending on taste

Total time: 1 hour
Serves 4

Heat oven to 400 F.

Pound chicken to thin flat pieces. Fold each piece around a chile and slice of cheese, secure with a toothpick.

In shallow dish, combine breadcrumbs, Parmesan and chili powder.

Roll each piece of chicken in oil, then roll in breadcrumb mixture.

Bake 40 minutes.

Submitted by: Carol McBride, The Island Packet

Favorite thing about this recipe: Easy and fast. Great with Mexican rice and salad and/or fruit.

Sesame Chicken Wings

- 40 chicken drumettes
- 1 cup mayonnaise
- 2 tsp dry mustard
- 2 tsp dried minced onions
- 1 cup breadcrumbs
- 1/2 cup sesame seeds

Total time: 1 hour
Serves 8-12

Heat oven to 375 F.

In bowl, mix together mayonnaise, dry mustard and dried onions.

In another bowl, mix together breadcrumbs and sesame seeds.

Coat 40 drumettes in mayonnaise mixture, then crumb mixture.

Place on baking sheet and bake for about 40 minutes.

Submitted by: Carol McBride, The Island Packet

Favorite thing about this recipe: Fast, easy, makes a lot, everyone loves.

Chicken Pot Pie

- 2 large chicken breasts
- 2 large chicken thighs
- 2 hard-boiled eggs, peeled and chopped
- 1 1/2 cup chicken broth
- 1 can cream of chicken soup
- 1 cup self-rising flour
- 1 cup milk (whole is preferable)
- 1/2 cup butter, melted

Total time: 1 hour, 15 minutes
Serves 4-6

Heat oven to 350 F.

Boil chicken, debone and shred. Arrange chicken pieces in bottom of buttered dish. Mix together eggs, chicken broth and cream of chicken soup. Pour over chicken.

Mix together flour, milk and melted butter. Pour over everything. Bake for 1 hour.

Submitted by: Margot Parrott, The Charlotte Observer

Favorite thing about this recipe: This chicken pot pie does not have any vegetables in it and is pure comfort food.

Side Dishes

Noodle Kugal

photo on page 95

Noodles

- 16 oz wide noodles
- 2 Tbsp butter
- 1 cup sugar
- 3 eggs, separated
- 1/4 cup raisins
- 1 apple, diced
- 1 tsp vanilla

Topping

- Cinnamon
- Butter

Total time: 1 hour, 30 minutes
Serves 6

Heat oven to 350 F.

Cook noodles and drain. Add butter and sugar. Mix in egg yolks, raisins, apples and vanilla.

Whip egg whites to stiff peaks. Fold into noodle mixture. Put into buttered square glass baking dish. Dot with butter on top and sprinkle cinnamon all over.

Bake for 1 hour.

Submitted by: Debbie Horvitz, National Winner — Miami Herald

Favorite thing about this recipe: You beat the egg whites and fold them in, making it a lighter noodle pudding. Also it is an old family favorite.

Scalloped Cabbage

- 4 cups cabbage, shredded
- 1/4 cup boiling water
- 2 eggs, slightly beaten
- 1/4 cup vinegar
- 1/2 cup mayonnaise
- 1/4 tsp salt
- 1 cup shredded cheddar cheese
- 8 oz salted potato chips, crushed

Total time: 45 minutes
Serves 4-6

Heat oven to 350 F.

Add cabbage to boiling water and cook 2 minutes, do not drain. Add eggs, vinegar, mayonnaise and salt, mix well.

Pour into greased 8x10 pan and bake 35 minutes, until mixture is bubbling.

Remove from oven and sprinkle cheese evenly on top, then add crushed potato chips on top of cheese. Bake additional 10 minutes, until cheese is browned.

Adjust vinegar, cheese and chips to taste. Keep liquid to a minimum in relation to the cabbage.

Submitted by: Gordon Hofstra, Local Winner — The Kansas City Star

Favorite thing about this recipe: Wonderful taste.

Chilled Cucumber Bisque

- 6 Tbsp butter, divided
- 2 medium onions, finely chopped
- 2 large cucumbers, peeled and finely chopped
- 3 cups chicken stock
- 2 Tbsp flour
- 2 egg yolks
- 1/2 cup heavy cream
- 1 medium cucumber, peeled and diced into 1/4-inch pieces
- Salt to taste
- White pepper, ground, to taste
- Parsley or chives, finely chopped

Total time: 3 hours, 45 minutes
Serves 6

In a heavy 3-quart saucepan, melt 4 Tbsp butter over medium heat. Stir in onions and cucumbers; cook for 5 minutes. Add the chicken stock and bring to a boil. Lower heat and simmer uncovered for 30 minutes.

Pour the soup into a sieve set over a large bowl and gently push the cooked vegetables through with the back of a spoon.

In the saucepan, melt the remaining 2 Tbsp of butter and stir in the flour. Pour in the pureed soup and, while whisking constantly, cook about 5 minutes, until the soup has thickened slightly.

In a small bowl, whisk the egg yolks and heavy cream. While continuing to whisk, very slowly add 1 cup of the hot soup. Then, slowly pour contents of the bowl into the remaining soup in the saucepan while continuously whisking. Simmer at low heat for 5 minutes.

Remove from heat, cool to room temperature, cover and refrigerate for 3 hours.

Before serving, stir in the diced cucumber, season with salt and pepper, and sprinkle with chopped chives or parsley.

Submitted by: Becky McGrady, Local Winner — Belleville News-Democrat

Favorite thing about this recipe: Cool, refreshing and deliciously silky.

Roasted Beet Salad with Walnuts and Dijon Vinaigrette

- 3 medium beets
- 1 Tbsp olive oil
- 1/2 cup walnuts or pecans, coarsely chopped
- 2 Tbsp honey
- 1 1/2 Tbsp Dijon mustard
- 3 Tbsp good quality red wine vinegar
- 1 1/2 Tbsp minced shallots
- Salt and pepper to taste
- 6 Tbsp vegetable or olive oil
- 12 oz mixed baby greens
- 3-4 oz goat cheese

Total time: 1 hour, 20 minutes
Serves 4-6

Roast the Beets

Heat oven to 425 F.

Scrub beets clean and trim stems. Rub with olive oil and wrap in foil. Roast in oven about 1 hour until tender.

Unwrap beets and let sit until cool enough to handle. Peel skin, then slice or dice as to your preference. This can be done the day before and stored in refrigerator.

Toast the Nuts

In pan over medium heat, toast nuts. Move constantly, until lightly browned, about 3 minutes.

Make Vinaigrette

Whisk together the honey, Dijon mustard, red wine vinegar, shallots, salt and pepper.

Whisking constantly, slowly add the oil in a steady stream to make an emulsion.

Serve

Place greens on individual plates and top with beets, nuts and goat cheese. Drizzle on vinaigrette.

Submitted by: Jeanne Stallings, Local Winner — The News & Observer (Raleigh)

Favorite thing about this recipe: Great blend of flavors and textures with a beautiful presentation.

Smoked Creamed Corn

photo on page 93

- 30 ears of corn, shucked
- 1/2 cup butter, plus additional for serving
- 2 tsp salt, plus additional for serving
- 1 tsp pepper, plus additional for serving
- 4 1/2 cups heavy cream

Total time: 3 hours
Serves 30

Corn

Heat smoker to "smoke" setting. Once heated, place corn on grates and close lid; smoke for 1 hour. If you do not have a smoker, grill on a barbecue for 30-45 minutes (turning 3 times throughout).

After one hour, increase the heat to 375 F for 30 minutes. Turn the corn halfway through.

Remove the corn and let cool to room temperature. Once cooled, slice kernels off the ears.

In a large pot, heat 1/2 cup butter and add corn kernels and saute on medium-low for 5 minutes, stirring occasionally.

Add 2 tsp salt, 1 tsp pepper, 4 1/2 cups cream, and increase heat to medium-high. Bring to a boil, stirring occasionally.

Reduce heat to medium-low heat, and let simmer. Stir occasionally for 35 minutes. The cream and butter will reduce and thicken. Finish with 1 tsp salt and 1/2 tsp pepper (or to taste).

Let cool completely and transfer to freezer storage containers. Freeze up to 6 months.

Serve

Thaw in refrigerator overnight. Heat oven to 325 F. Transfer desired amount to a baking dish and top with a few dollops of butter. Cover and bake 30-45 minutes, stirring occasionally.

Submitted by: Allison Barker, Local Winner — The Olympian

Favorite thing about this recipe: This is a holiday side dish favorite! It's got a nice smoky flavor that doesn't overpower the natural sweetness of the corn. I like making a large batch and freezing it in smaller containers to use throughout the holiday season.

Shaye's Super Stuffing

- 1 box or bag seasoned bread stuffing
- 1 box or bag cornbread stuffing
- 1/2 cup celery, chopped
- 1/4 cup onion, diced
- 1/2 cup pecans, chopped
- 1/2 cup walnuts, chopped
- 1 Tbsp dried sage
- 1 lb uncooked bulk sausage
- 1/2 large jar apple sauce
- 1/2 large can crushed pineapple
- 1 small jar peach preserves
- 1 cup chicken or turkey stock
- 1/2 cup butter, melted

Total time: 1 hour, 30 minutes
Serves 8-10

Heat oven to 350 F.

In large mixing bowl, combine all ingredients and spread in 9x13 baking dish sprayed with nonstick spray. Bake for about an hour or until sausage is cooked.

Amounts can adjusted to personal taste; to achieve desired moisture and consistency.

Submitted by: Shaye Yarnell, Local Winner — The Tribune (San Luis Obispo)

Favorite thing about this recipe: I love the simplicity of this recipe and people who don't normally like dressing, love it.

Squash and Apple Bake

- 1/2 cup brown sugar
- 1 Tbsp flour
- 1/2 cup rolled oats (not instant)
- 1 tsp salt
- 1/2 tsp cinnamon
- 1/4 cup butter, melted
- 3-4 large apples, sliced
- 1 medium butternut squash, cut into small chunks
- 4 Tbsp butter, sliced

Total time: 1 hour, 15 minutes
Serves 6-8

Heat oven to 350 F.

In medium bowl, combine brown sugar, flour, oats, salt and cinnamon together. Add melted butter and mix together.

Arrange cut apples and squash in baking dish. Sprinkle sugar mixture on top and throughout. Dot with butter slices.

Cover and bake for 50-60 minutes or until golden brown.

Submitted by: Kathy Hocker,
The Charlotte Observer

Favorite thing about this recipe: Delicious way to make squash and use the bounty of the fall harvest.

Cranberry Surprise

- Two 14-oz cans jellied or whole cranberry sauce
- 15-oz can mandarin oranges
- 20-oz can crushed pineapple, drained
- 1 small package black cherry Jell-O mix
- 1/2 cup pecan pieces

Total time: 20 minutes
Serves 10

In large bowl, mix all ingredients well. Refrigerate at least 1 hour. Serve.

You can halve this recipe if you want, but it keeps well for 4 or 5 days and is wonderful with any protein.

Submitted by: Linda Warrington, Local Winner — The Wichita Eagle

Favorite thing about this recipe: Easy and delicious.

Garden Harvest Delight

photo on page 99
- 2 Tbsp butter
- 2 Tbsp olive oil
- 1 cup onions, thinly sliced
- 2 cloves garlic, finely diced
- 1 cup red or green pepper, thinly sliced
- 2 cups zucchini, cut in 1/4-inch slices
- 6 button mushrooms, quartered
- 3 medium tomatoes, peeled and sliced
- 1 heaping tsp salt
- 1/4 tsp pepper
- 1 tsp dry basil or 2 1/2 tsp fresh basil, finely chopped
- 1 Tbsp cornstarch
- 1 Tbsp cold water
- 1 Tbsp parsley, finely chopped
- Parmesan cheese

Total time: 30 minutes
Serves 4-6

In large saucepan or Dutch oven on medium heat, add butter and olive oil. Saute onions, garlic and peppers. Cook until soft.

Add zucchini, mushrooms, tomatoes, salt, pepper and basil. Simmer on low about 10 minutes, stirring occasionally until vegetables are tender and juice is slightly reduced.

Dissolve cornstarch in cold water, and stir into vegetables and simmer until thickened.

Pour into an 8x8 baking dish. Sprinkle with parsley and Parmesan cheese.

Shortly before serving, put under broiler until cheese bubbles. Serve hot.

Submitted by: Barbara Costanti, The News Tribune (Tacoma)

Favorite thing about this recipe: It is made with all fresh ingredients and things commonly grown in home gardens.

Rhubarb Barbecue Sauce

- 6 stalks rhubarb, cubed
- 4 cups brown sugar
- 1/4 cup yellow mustard
- 4 cups ketchup
- Dash of salt

Total time: 45 minutes
Yields 4 cups

In saucepan, combine all ingredients and simmer together until rhubarb is tender.

Submitted by: Nancy Boat,
The Bellingham Herald

Favorite thing about this recipe: Tangy yet sweet, use on barbecue meats.

Kitty's Punjabi Rice

photo on page 100

- 1 medium yellow onion, diced
- 1 Tbsp olive oil
- 1 tsp minced garlic
- 3/4 tsp salt
- 1 tsp ground cumin
- 1 Roma tomato, diced
- 1 medium or small gold potato, thinly sliced
- 1/2 cup basmati rice
- 1/8 tsp garam masala

Total time: 30 minutes
Serves 2-4

In a medium or large pot, place onion with olive oil, add minced garlic and fry until onions are clear.

Add salt, ground cumin, diced tomato and potato, mix and fry 1-2 minutes more.

Wash rice. Add rice and garam masala. Add a tiny bit more than 1 cup of water and cover with lid after brought to slight boil.

Turn down temperature to low and let simmer for 15 minutes.

Take rice off the heat and let sit for 10 minutes, still covered — do not lift the lid! Serve and enjoy!

Submitted by: Kaitlin Menchaca,
The Bellingham Herald

Favorite thing about this recipe: In India there aren't any recipes or measuring cups. This is my mother-in-law's dish and I would watch her cook and made up this recipe as a mock of hers. It's fast and simple, I just keep a lot of onions and tomatoes and make it daily for my husband.

From top: Beef Cacciatore (page 58); Pan-Seared Salmon with
Sauteed Mushrooms and Dirty Rice (page 46)

Clockwise from right: Bean Tortilla (page 25); Seared Flat Iron Steak with Horseradish Cream (page 62); J's Slow Cooker Lasagna (page 48)

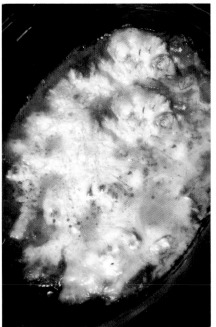

From top: Creamy Turkey and Rice Soup
(page 34); Chicken Cacciatore (page 49)

Clockwise from opposite: Tater Tot-Topped Chicken Pot Pie (page 52); Deconstructed Eggplant Cannelloni with Cashew Crema (page 13); Dr Pepper Pulled Brisket (page 14)

Clockwise from above: Pan-Seared Trout with Field Peas (page 43); Magic German Apple Pancakes (page 65); Hunter's Finger Steaks (page 28)

Clockwise from opposite top left:
Margarita Salmon (page 61); Greg's King
Ranch Pot Pie Casserole (page 56);
Speckled Trout a la Meunier (page 22);
Shrimp and Blue Cheese Tortilla (page 37);
Salmon Sliders (page 36); Oven Fried Fish
(page 20)

From top: Easy Spicy
Orange Chicken (page 38);
Squeaky Pork and Beans
(page 53)

Clockwise from top left: Terrebonne Cajun Cabbage (page 21); Potato Something Else (page 33); Shrimp Napoleon (page 9)

Clockwise from above: Country Sweet and Sour Green Beans with Bacon (page 115); Six Boy Taco (page 68); Campfire Veggies (page 117)

From top: Roasted Asparagus Romano (page 119); Smoked Creamed Corn (page 77)

From top: Pumpkin Soup (page 161); Zucchini and Squash Au Gratin (page 129)

Clockwise from top left: Outta Sight Stuffed Celery (page 136); Noodle Kugal (page 74); Salmon Raisin Spread (page 148)

Clockwise from opposite top left: Broccoli Supreme Casserole (page 162); Fancy Green Beans (page 160); Creamy Crunchy Cucumber Pea Salad (page 168); Potato and Sweet Potato Kees (page 165); Jeff's Pig Roll (page 116)

From top: Farro with Spring
Vegetables and Creme Fraiche
(page 163); Nanny's Challah
Bread (page 152)

Clockwise from top: Garden Harvest Delight (page 79); Julie's Apple Butter (page 155); Granny Pat's Mashed Potatoes (page 141)

Clockwise from above: Kitty's Punjabi Rice
(page 80); Turkey Stuffing (page 153);
Sticky Beans (page 164); Tuscan Picnic
Sardine Pie (page 147)

Clockwise from opposite: Tastin' Jamaican Shark Bites Salad (page 151); Stuffed Squash Blossoms (page 118); Red and White Tomato Salad (page 113); Zucchini and Carrots with Pancetta (page 154)

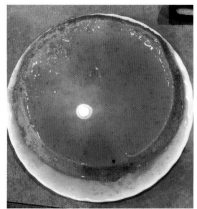

Clockwise from top left: Apple, Banana, Cranberry, Pecan Morning Bread (page 182); Pumpkin Flan (page 173); Strawberry Pizza (page 189); Triple Treat Cocoa Cakes (page 193)

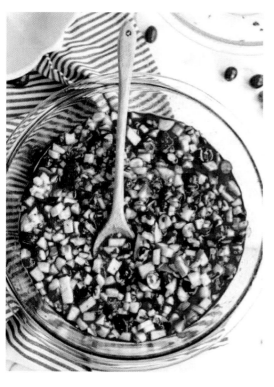

From top: Cranberry Jell-O Salad (page 201);
Marvelous Macaroons (page 207)

Clockwise from above: Boy Scout Cobbler
(page 199); Mini Caramel Filled Pumpkin
Cakes with Salted Almonds (page 188);
Bourbon Cinnamon Pecan Bundt Cake
(page 172); Cheese Flan (page 203)

Clockwise from above: Chocolate Bourbon Pecan Pie (page 183); Apple Pie Squares (page 176); Lemon and Toffee Chip Ice Cream (page 204); Pistachio Nut Cookies (page 190); Coconut Cream Pie with Chocolate Drizzle (page 202); Black Forest Cheesecake (page 187)

Clockwise from opposite: Double Chocolate Cream Pie (page 196); Marie's Biscotti (page 195); Lavish Latte Lava Cake (page 197)

From top: Aunt June's Banana Pudding (page 176); Pumpkin Cake (page 191)

Voodoo Pasta Salad

- 2 1/2 cups uncooked penne pasta
- 1 1/2-2 cups mayonnaise (or to taste)
- 1 1/2 tsp salt
- 1 1/2 tsp black pepper
- 1 1/2 tsp minced garlic
- 1 1/2 Tbsp ground cumin
- 2 1/2 cups cooked bay shrimp, or frozen bay shrimp (sometimes called salad shrimp) thawed according to package directions
- 3 Tbsp jalapeño peppers, minced
- 1/4 cup cilantro, chopped
- 1/2 cup yellow bell pepper, julienned (matchstick-size pieces)
- 1/2 cup red bell pepper, julienned (matchstick-size pieces)
- 1/2 cup green onion
- 1 cup Parmesan cheese, grated

Total time: 1 hour
Serves 8-10

Cook pasta according to package directions; drain and let cool.

In medium bowl, stir together mayonnaise, salt, pepper, garlic and cumin.

In a large bowl, toss together pasta, shrimp (optional), jalapeños, cilantro, bell peppers and green onions. Add mayonnaise mixture, toss to combine.

Chill for 20 minutes. Top with Parmesan to serve.

Submitted by: Linda Wood, Belleville News-Democrat

Favorite thing about this recipe: So versatile. Can be main dish or side dish depending on shrimp. Most requested recipe at gatherings.

Red and White Tomato Salad

photo on page 103

- 1 large tomato, sliced
- 4 onion slices, separated into rings
- 1 Tbsp olive oil
- 1/3 cup white vinegar
- 1/3 cup water
- 2/3 cup sugar
- 1/4 Tbsp salt
- 1/4 Tbsp pepper

Total time: 40 minutes
Serves 2-4

In a serving bowl, layer the tomato and onion slices.

In a small bowl, whisk together remaining ingredients. Drizzle the dressing over the tomatoes and onions and allow to marinate 30 minutes before serving.

Note: These are also very tasty served on a sandwich or served with mozzarella cheese cubes.

Submitted by: Nancy Posey, Belleville News-Democrat

Favorite thing about this recipe: Tasty and quick to prepare.

Sweet Onion Pie

- 1 1/2 sleeves Ritz Crackers
- 1 cup butter, divided
- 4 cups onions, thinly sliced
- 1 cup sour cream
- 2 eggs, lightly beaten
- 1 cup cheddar cheese, shredded

Total time: 45 minutes
Serves 6-8

Heat oven to 350 F.

In food processor, add crackers and finely crush. Add 1/2 cup of melted butter and mix.

Press crumb mixture into 9-inch pan, forming crust.

In frying pan, melt 1/2 cup of butter and saute onions until translucent. Add onions to crust.

In bowl, mix sour cream and eggs until blended and spoon over the onions.

Sprinkle cheese over pie and bake for 30 minutes.

Submitted by: Linda Wood, Belleville News-Democrat

Favorite thing about this recipe: Unique side dish.

Yellow Squash Casserole

- 8 small yellow squash, cut in 1-inch pieces
- 1 cup onion, chopped
- 1/2 cup green pepper, chopped
- 4 Tbsp butter, melted
- 1 cup shredded cheese
- 1 egg, well beaten
- 2 cups bread or cracker crumbs (1 for mixture and 1 for topping)

Total time: 1 hour, 30 minutes
Serves 4

Heat oven to 350 F.

In skillet, saute squash, onion and green peppers until tender and cool slightly.

In large bowl, mix butter, cheese, egg, 1 cup crumbs, squash, onion and green pepper. If mixture is too watery, you can add additional crumbs.

Pour into buttered 8x8 baking dish.

Top with remaining crumbs and bake for 30-45 minutes.

Submitted by: Maxine Ramsay, Sun Herald

Favorite thing about this recipe: It is a tasty vegetable dish and nutritious.

Country Sweet and Sour Green Beans with Bacon

photo on page 92

- 4 cups fresh green beans, cut
- 4 slices thick-sliced bacon, cut into pieces (Note: The easiest way to cut bacon is with kitchen shears.)
- 1/4 cup onion, chopped
- 2 Tbsp sugar
- 2 Tbsp white vinegar
- 1/2 tsp salt
- 1/4 tsp black pepper

Total time: 30 minutes
Serves 4

In pan, cover green beans with water and cook until soft. Drain and put back in the pan. Set aside.

In skillet, cook bacon on medium heat until almost crisp. Remove bacon from pan. Using a small dish covered with a paper towel (secure with rubber band), strain bacon grease.

Wipe out skillet.

In skillet, put a small amount of the bacon grease and cook onion on medium heat until soft. Add sugar, vinegar, salt, pepper and bacon into the pan with the onions. Cook on medium heat for 2 minutes.

Stir in cooked green beans and stir mixture on medium heat for 5 minutes or until beans are hot and coated with the sugar/vinegar/bacon mixture.

Submitted by: Barbara McKinley, Centre Daily Times

Favorite thing about this recipe: A different way to make green beans.

Jacqueline's Trail Mix

- Pistachios
- Dried cranberries
- Sunflower seeds
- Pumpkin seeds
- Almonds
- Cashews
- Dried strawberries
- Raisins
- Dried cherries
- Prunes

Total time: 20 minutes
Serves 1 or more

Pour 1/2 cup (more or less) of all ingredients. Adding or omitting for taste is allowed.

Add oats or cornflakes if desired.

Pour into zip-close bags.

Submitted by: Jacqueline Jones, The Telegraph (Macon)

Favorite thing about this recipe: Tasty! Natural.

Jeff's Pig Roll

photo on page 96

- Sweet peppers
- Cream Cheese
- Bacon

Total time: 30 minutes
Serves 1 or more

Heat oven to 375 F.

Wash the peppers; remove tops and seeds.

Stuff each pepper with cream cheese.

Roll 1/2 or whole bacon slice around each pepper, according to your desire.

On baking sheet lined with foil, arrange wrapped peppers.

Bake for 30 minutes. Finish with a 5-minute broil.

Submitted by: Jeffrey Jones, The Charlotte Observer

Favorite thing about this recipe: Crowd pleaser.

Campfire Veggies

photo on page 92

- 1 cup onion, sliced
- 2 cups Brussels sprouts, halved
- 1 cup baby carrots
- Olive oil
- 2 tsp all-purpose seasoning

Total time: 1 hour
Serves 1 or more

In cast-iron skillet, add all ingredients, using just enough olive oil to ensure it doesn't stick.

Cook over campfire, stirring every 10 minutes with a wooden spoon so it doesn't stick. Add more olive oil as needed. Cook until fork tender.

Submitted by: Dawn Bedenbaugh, The State

Favorite thing about this recipe: Cooking and staying warm!!

Prune Bread

- 2 cups sugar
- 3 eggs
- 1 cup vegetable oil
- 1 cup prunes, cooked and pitted
- 2 cups flour
- 1 tsp cloves
- 1 tsp salt
- 1 tsp cinnamon
- 1 tsp baking soda
- 1/2 tsp nutmeg
- 3/4 cups buttermilk

Total time: 1 hour, 15 minutes
Yields 1 loaf

Heat oven to 350 F.

Grease bottom of loaf pan and line with wax paper.

Mix together sugar, eggs, oil and prunes.

Add dry ingredients, alternating with buttermilk.

Bake about 1 hour.

Submitted by: Van Patty Oosbree, The Fresno Bee

Favorite thing about this recipe: Made up by my mother-in-law who passed away in 1977. It was a family favorite and has been passed through the family for years.

Stuffed Squash Blossoms

photo on page 103

- 4 oz goat cheese, room temperature
- 4 oz ricotta cheese, room temperature
- 2 cloves garlic, grated
- 2 Tbsp capers, drained and minced
- 1 tsp kosher salt
- 16 squash blossoms, remove pistil, stem and any sharp green parts
- Tempura batter mix
- Oil for frying
- Balsamic vinegar reduction

Total time: 1 hour
Serves 4

In bowl, mix goat and ricotta cheese with garlic, capers and kosher salt. Put mixture into a zip-close bag and cut one corner off.

Pipe in mixture into each blossom, you don't need much in each. Note: You can refrigerate blossoms at this point until ready to cook.

Make a tempura batter using package instructions.

Dip blossoms into batter, shaking off excess.

Deep-fry in about 2 inches of oil, turning once.

Serve with a balsamic vinegar reduction.

Submitted by: Daniel Houts,
The Fresno Bee

Favorite thing about this recipe: A springtime farmer's market treat.

Banana Salsa

- 3 bananas
- 3 Roma tomatoes, diced
- 1 cup onion, diced
- 1/4 cup green onions, diced
- 1/4 cup green peppers, diced
- Salt and pepper to taste
- Pinch of parsley and cilantro to taste
- Sour cream, 1 spoonful in case acidity is a problem or for extra taste

Total time: 25 minutes
Serves 6-8

In mixing bowl, smash 2 bananas. Dice the last banana.

Go down the list, adding all other ingredients (except the diced banana) into the smashed banana with spatula.

When you have a consistency you like, add the diced bananas and give one final stir and voilá!

Banana salsa to be served over grilled cheese sandwiches or with crackers.

Submitted by: Lasondra Huggins,
Fort Worth Star-Telegram

Favorite thing about this recipe: It is versatile.

Roasted Asparagus Romano

photo on page 93

- 1 lb green asparagus, ends trimmed
- 1/2 cup Italian-flavored breadcrumbs
- 1 tsp garlic powder
- 1/2 cup Parmesan cheese, grated
- Salt and pepper to taste (if the cheese is very salty do not add salt)
- Olive oil

Total time: 30 minutes
Serves 6

Heat oven to 425 F.

Arrange the asparagus evenly on a rimmed baking sheet. Cover them with the breadcrumbs, garlic, Parmesan cheese, salt and pepper. Sprinkle the asparagus with water, then drizzle olive oil over them.

Place it in the oven for 15-20 minutes or until tender-crisp. The cooking time can be reduced if you like your asparagus crisp. Serve immediately.

Submitted by: Nicholas Verna, The News & Observer (Raleigh)

Favorite thing about this recipe: The asparagus stays crispy tender and the salty Romano cheese adds a umami punch that brings out the flavor of the asparagus.

Holiday Sweet Potatoes

- 3 medium sweet potatoes, peeled and cut into large wedges
- 1 tsp cinnamon
- Pinch of salt
- 1/4 clove
- Fresh nutmeg, grated
- 4 Tbsp butter
- 1 lemon wedge
- Large marshmallows

Total time: 55 minutes
Serves 6-8

Heat oven to 350 F.

In pot, boil sweet potato wedges about 20 minutes. Drain.

Place cooked potatoes into casserole dish and sprinkle with cinnamon, salt and nutmeg. Squeeze lemon juice over top. Bake for 25 minutes.

Add marshmallows on top and broil until browned, careful not to burn.

Submitted by: Kelley Cates, Fort Worth Star-Telegram

Favorite thing about this recipe: It's yummy.

Potato Salad

- Russet potatoes
- Vinegar
- Boiled eggs
- Celery salt
- Sweet pickles, cubed
- Stuffed olives, sliced
- Mayonnaise

Total time: 1 hour
Serves 1 or more

Boil russet potatoes until fork tender.

Cool and peel potatoes, slice in half and add 1 Tbsp vinegar to each half.

Continue to cool and cut into cubes.

Add cubed boiled eggs salted with celery salt (1 egg for each potato).

Add cubed sweet pickles (about one sweet pickle to each potato).

Add stuffed olives and mayonnaise to taste.

Submitted by: Carole Duffield, Fort Worth Star-Telegram

Favorite thing about this recipe: The vinegar adds the right zest to the salad.

Seriously Stupid Rolls

Rolls

- 1 package dry yeast
- 1/4 cup lukewarm water
- 2 1/2 cups flour
- 1/4 cup sugar
- 1 tsp salt
- 1/2 cup butter
- 1 cup creamed cottage cheese
- 1 egg

Filling

- 3 Tbsp butter, melted
- 3/4 cup brown sugar
- 1/4 tsp salt
- 1/2 tsp almond extract
- 1/2 tsp vanilla extract
- 1/4 tsp orange extract
- 2/3 cup nuts, chopped

Total time: 2 hours, 30 minutes
Serves 12

Dissolve yeast in water.

Sift flour, sugar and salt together and cut butter in. Add cottage cheese, egg and yeast to flour mixture.

Roll dough into a 14-inch square.

In separate bowl, combine filling ingredients. Spread filling over dough and roll up like a jelly roll.

Slice into 1-inch slices and place on a greased baking sheet.

Cover with towel and allow 2 hours to double in size.

Heat oven to 425 F. Bake for 15-20 minutes until golden brown.

Submitted by: Brian Harp, Fort Worth Star-Telegram

Favorite thing about this recipe: It's delicious and easy to prepare. Like a cinnamon roll but with almond goodness.

My Salsa

- 1 can chopped tomatoes
- 1 can RO*TEL Diced Tomatoes and Green Chilies
- 1/2 onion, chopped
- 1 jalapeño, chopped
- Salt and pepper
- Garlic (powder or fresh)

Total time: 1 hour, 15 minutes
Serves 2-4

In blender, add both cans of tomatoes and pulse a few times. Don't turn into liquid.

In pot, add tomatoes and remaining ingredients. Bring to boil and lower to simmer. Simmer for 1 hour, stirring regularly.

Add seasoning to taste. Let cool.

Grab a bag of chips and enjoy.

Submitted by: Dale Hicks, Fort Worth Star-Telegram

Favorite thing about this recipe: Flavor.

Tangy Dip/Salad Dressing

- 4 Tbsp mayonnaise (*not* Miracle Whip)
- 2 Tbsp sour cream
- 1-2 Tbsp balsamic white vinegar (or to taste)
- 2-3 Tbsp sweetener (or to taste; sucralose or other zero calorie artificial sweetener)
- Fresh ground black pepper

Total time: 15 minutes
Serves 1 or more

In medium mixing bowl or container, combine all ingredients.

After all ingredients appear to be moist, beat the ingredients with a large spoon until ingredients are smooth and creamy.

Keep in an air-tight container in the refrigerator. Use as a dip, salad dressing, fish condiment, roast beef condiment or anything you feel would be enhanced by these ingredients.

Submitted by: Kay Jones, Fort Worth Star-Telegram

Favorite thing about this recipe: Easy to make and easy to keep.

Rosie's World Famous Italian Meatballs — A Special Thanksgiving Treat for Dogs

- 1 lb ground turkey or chicken
- 10 oz frozen spinach, cooked and drained
- 2-3 carrots, finely chopped
- 1/2 red pepper, ribs and seeds removed, finely chopped
- 1 egg, lightly beaten
- 1/3 cup Parmesan (shaker type ok)
- 1/4 cup dried parsley
- 2 Tbsp dried oregano
- 2 tsp turmeric

Total time: 3 hours
Yields 48 treats

In large bowl, combine all ingredients and thoroughly mix. Place in the refrigerator for a couple of hours to chill.

Heat oven to 350 F.

Using a 3/4-inch cookie scoop, form into balls and place on parchment- or silicone mat-lined cookie sheet.

Bake for 45-50 minutes.

Cool completely and store in airtight container in the fridge for 2 weeks, or freeze for up to 2 months.

Thaw before treating. Your dog will love you even more when you make these meatballs!

Submitted by: Mark Renfro, Fort Worth Star-Telegram

Favorite thing about this recipe: Rosie follows me to the kitchen and is a constant companion until the treats are cool enough to eat. This recipe is wonderfully forgiving. Have some leftover green beans you'd like to use up? Chop and toss them in the bowl. Include that leftover bit of flax seed. Kale instead of spinach? OK. Feel free to include any vegetable your dog likes — just keep the addition in proportion to the whole and watch the cooking time to avoid overcooking.

Side Dish Spaghetti

- 3/4 lb bacon
- 2 small cans Hunt's tomato sauce
- Salt
- Pepper
- 2 Tbsp sugar
- 1 box spaghetti

Total time: 30 minutes
Serves 8

Fry bacon and cut into small pieces. Add tomato sauce and sugar to bacon. Do not drain grease. Salt and pepper to taste. Cook spaghetti and drain. Mix sauce and spaghetti and serve in large bowl.

Submitted by: Judy Winnenberg, The Island Packet

Favorite thing about this recipe: The smiles on my family's faces when I make it!

Corn Casserole

- 1 can cream corn
- 1 cup Bisquick
- 1 egg, beaten slightly
- 2 tsp oleo (margarine), melted
- 1/2 cup milk
- 16 oz shredded cheese
- 4-oz can chopped green chilies

Total time: 35 minutes
Serves 12

Heat oven to 350 F.
   Mix all ingredients together. Pour into greased 9x13 pan.
   Bake for 30 minutes.

Submitted by: Brenda Stafford, Fort Worth Star-Telegram

Favorite thing about this recipe: The taste is amazing.

Sweet Potato Casserole

Casserole

- 3 cups sweet potatoes, cooked and mashed
- 1 cup sugar
- 2 eggs
- 4 Tbsp butter
- 1/2 cup milk
- 1 tsp vanilla
- 1 tsp orange zest

Topping

- 1 cup brown sugar (not packed)
- 1 cup pecans, chopped
- 1 cup coconut
- 1/4 cup flour
- 1/4 cup butter, melted

Total time: 1 hour, 30 minutes
Serves 12-15

Heat oven to 350 F.

In food processor or with fork, mix topping ingredients.

Mix casserole ingredients with mixer. Spread into greased 2-quart baking dish.

Place topping over sweet potato mixture. Bake uncovered for 30 minutes or until top is slightly toasted.

Submitted by: Linda Wood, The Kansas City Star

Favorite thing about this recipe: It's so tasty, it could be a pie too.

Basil Bread (Bread Machine)

- 1 cup, plus 2 Tbsp water
- 1/2 tsp salt
- 2 Tbsp granulated sugar
- 2 Tbsp olive oil
- 1 Tbsp dry milk powder (optional)
- 3 cups bread flour
- 1 Tbsp dried basil
- 1-1/2 tsp instant or bread-machine yeast

Total time: 4 hours
Yields one 1 1/2 lb loaf

Check bread machine to make sure stirring paddle is in place. Place ingredients in bread pan in the order specified by the maker of your machine. (If unknown, the order of ingredients is probably good.) Process on the white bread or regular setting. Use light crust setting. Remove when machine signals the bread is ready and let cool on a rack. Slice or tear apart to serve.

Submitted by: Eileen Chase, The Kansas City Star

Favorite thing about this recipe: Nice taste of olive oil and basil.

Double Choke Salad

- 1 jar quartered artichokes
- 1/4 cup vegetable oil
- 1/2 tsp dried thyme
- 1/4 tsp garlic powder
- Mayonnaise
- Salad fixings of your choice: lettuce, spinach, tomatoes, green onions, cucumbers, etc.

Total time: 30 minutes
Serves 1 or more

Note

Some artichoke brands may have oil in the jar already, so check ingredients.

Make the dressing: In a large bowl, pour 2 Tbsp of the liquid from the artichokes and the vegetable oil. Add thyme and garlic powder. Take a wire whisk and dip it into mayonnaise so as to take on a small amount, say 1/4 tsp. (The mayo will emulsify the dressing so the oil and water do not separate.) Whisk the dressing well.

Prepare the salad as usual, washing, cutting and tossing the ingredients in the large bowl. At the end, add the amount of quartered artichokes you desire to the salad and stir gently.

Submitted by: Eileen Chase, The Kansas City Star

Favorite thing about this recipe:
Sophisticated new taste.

Frank's Saucy Barbecue Beans

- 6 slices bacon, cut into 1/2-inch pieces
- 1 1/2 onion, chopped
- 1/2 green pepper, chopped
- 1/4 cup brown sugar
- 1 1/2 Tbsp Worcestershire sauce
- 1/4 tsp cayenne pepper
- 2 Tbsp yellow mustard
- 6 Tbsp barbecue sauce
- 1/2 cup ketchup
- 1/2 tsp salt (or to taste)
- 1/2 tsp celery salt
- 1 Tbsp black pepper
- 1 Tbsp garlic powder
- 1 Tbsp chili powder
- 2 Tbsp tomato paste
- Six 15-oz cans pork and beans, drained of excess liquid
- Great to add scraps of brisket or smoked meat if available

Total time: 4 hours
Serves 18-20

In skillet or Dutch oven, cook bacon. Remove bacon and drain most of the grease. Cook onion and green pepper in remaining grease until translucent and softened. Add the bacon and remaining ingredients (through tomato paste) back to pan and heat together. Add beans and continue to heat until warmed throughout

You can put together all ingredients except the beans ahead of time and refrigerate for several days, then merely add to the beans and heat when ready to serve. With some liquid removed from the beans, oven baking is not necessary.

Submitted by: Frank Newkirk, The Kansas City Star

Favorite thing about this recipe:
Complements grilled food, easy prep.

Green Beans Chinese Style

- 1 lb fresh green beans
- Vegetable cooking spray
- 1 tsp vegetable oil
- 1 tsp ginger root, peeled and minced
- 1 clove garlic, minced
- 2 Tbsp water
- 1 Tbsp low-sodium soy sauce
- 1 tsp cornstarch
- 1/2 tsp brown sugar
- 1/2 tsp dark sesame oil
- 1/4 tsp crushed red pepper

Total time: 30 minutes
Serves 8

Wash beans, trim ends and remove strings. Arrange beans in a vegetable steamer, and place over boiling water. Cover and steam for 5 minutes. Drain and plunge into cold water; drain again.

Coat a large nonstick skillet with cooking spray. Add vegetable oil and place over medium-high heat until hot. Add ginger and garlic; saute for 30 seconds. Add beans; saute 5 minutes or until heated through.

In a bowl, combine water with soy sauce, cornstarch, brown sugar, sesame oil and red pepper; stir well. Add to beans. Cook 30 seconds, or until thoroughly heated, stirring constantly.

Submitted by: Pauline Martin, The Kansas City Star

Favorite thing about this recipe:
The unusual taste for green beans.

Sausage Bacon Bites

- 3/4 lb sliced bacon
- Two 6.4-oz packages Brown 'N Serve Original Sausage Links
- 1/2 cup brown sugar

Total time: 4 hours, 30 minutes
(or more depending on refrigeration time)
Serves 6

Cut bacon strips in half width-wise. Place 1/2 of brown sugar in a shallow baking dish and roll sausages and bacon strips in brown sugar until coated. Place bacon around sausage and secure with toothpicks. Cover and refrigerate for 4-24 hours.

Heat oven to 350 F. Bake for 30-45 minutes, until bacon is crisp, turning once.

Submitted by: Thomas Arnhold, The Kansas City Star

Favorite thing about this recipe: Easy to make it.

Zucchini and Squash Au Gratin

photo on page 94

- Olive oil
- 1 onion, chopped
- 4-6 cloves garlic, minced
- 3 yellow squash, sliced into 1/4-inch thick slices
- 3 green zucchini, sliced into 1/4-inch thick slices
- 2 cups panko (breadcrumbs)
- 3 Tbsp butter
- 1 1/2 cups Parmesan, shredded
- 1 1/2 cups smoked Gouda, shredded
- Fresh herbs or herbes de Provence
- Salt and pepper
- Red pepper flakes
- 2-3 cups cream or half-and-half
- 5-6 tomatoes, sliced into 1/4-inch thick slices

Total time: 1 hour, 30 minutes
Serves 8

Heat oven to 450 F.

Use olive oil to saute the onion until translucent, then add the garlic and saute.

Saute zucchini and squash into onion mixture until al dente.

Drain mixture to remove excess water.

In a bowl, add the panko, melted butter, 1/3 of shredded cheeses, herbes de Provence (or fresh herbs), salt, pepper and red pepper flakes and mix.

Take zucchini and squash mixture and put back in saute pan. Fold in remaining 2/3 of cheeses, plus cream (enough to coat it well).

In a 9x13 baking dish, rub olive oil all over.

Add mixture to baking dish.

Then layer sliced tomatoes over the top (feel free to salt and pepper tomatoes a little if you would like).

Then sprinkle breadcrumb mixture all over the top of the tomatoes.

Bake for 16-20 minutes.

If necessary, broil for 5 minutes to make top crispier. Let cool for 10 minutes then serve.

Submitted by: Maija Diethelm, The Kansas City Star

Favorite thing about this recipe: I took my grandmother's recipe and added my own flair to it. This is a traditional southern France dish called Provençal Vegetable Tian.

Tom's Baked Beans

- 1 lb sausage
- 4-6 strips bacon
- 1/2 lb ground beef
- 3 Tbsp vinegar
- 1/2 cup ketchup
- 1 tsp dry mustard
- 1 Tbsp liquid smoke
- 3/4 cup brown sugar
- 1 onion, chopped
- 1/2 tsp garlic powder
- 15-oz can kidney beans, drained
- 15-oz can baked beans
- 15-oz can lima beans, drained

Total time: 1 hour
Serves 8-10

Heat oven to 350 F.

Fry sausage; remove from pan and crumble. Fry bacon and crumble. Brown ground beef and add remaining ingredients. Cook until blended.

Place all mixture into casserole and bake for 40 minutes.

Note

You can add or substitute chili beans, black beans, pinto beans, northern beans or garbanzo beans. You can also add cooked bacon, kielbasa, pulled pork, barbecued brisket or other desired meat.

Submitted by: Thomas Arnhold, The Kansas City Star

Favorite thing about this recipe: The variety of beans.

Fig and Port Mustard

- 1 1/4 cups dried figs, chopped
- 1/2 cup port wine
- 1/4 cup mustard seed (white or yellow)
- 2 Tbsp Champagne vinegar

Total time: 1 hour, 30 minutes
Yields 12 oz

In a bowl, combine figs and port and let stand 1 hour.

Blend or process fig mixture with mustard seeds and vinegar until combined.

Store covered in glass jar.

Submitted by: Thomas Arnhold, The Kansas City Star

Favorite thing about this recipe: The flavor.

Cranberry Salad

- Two 3-oz boxes strawberry Jell-O
- 1 cup hot water
- 3/4-1 cup sugar
- 2 cups raw cranberries, ground
- 1 orange, cut into small pieces
- Orange peel, grated
- 1 cup crushed pineapple, drained
- 1 apple, cut up into small pieces
- 1/2 cup pecans, chopped
- 2-5 celery stalks, cut into small pieces

Total time: 1 hour
Serves 8-10

Dissolve Jell-O in hot water. Then add all ingredients, pour into dish and refrigerate.

Submitted by: Elizabeth Burton, The Kansas City Star

Favorite thing about this recipe: It's my Grandma's recipe.

Nana's Cabbage Noodles

- 12 oz farfalle pasta
- 2 Tbsp vegetable oil
- 1 head cabbage, finely shredded
- 1 1/2 tsp salt
- 3/4 tsp black pepper
- 1 Tbsp sugar, brown or white

Total time: 25 minutes
Serves 6

Boil pasta in salted water, drain and set aside.

In Dutch oven, saute oil, cabbage, salt, pepper and sugar until lightly browned. Add pasta to cabbage mixture.

Submitted by: Teede Stipich, The Kansas City Star

Favorite thing about this recipe: It was my Hungarian grandma's.

Spiced Mustard Greens

- 1 lb fresh mustard greens, chopped
- 9 oz fresh spinach, chopped
- 4 cloves garlic, minced
- 2-inch piece fresh ginger, peeled and minced
- 2 serrano chilis, seeded and chopped
- 1 tsp kosher salt (or to taste)
- 1 tsp dark brown sugar
- 1 Tbsp fine cornmeal

Spiced Butter Sauce

- 2 tsp ghee or unsalted butter
- 1/2 tsp chili powder
- 1-inch piece fresh ginger, peeled and cut into strips

Total time: 45-50 minutes
Serves 4

In a heavy pan, bring 1 1/4 cups water to a boil. Add the mustard greens, spinach, garlic, ginger and chilis. Bring back to a boil, reduce the heat to low, cover and cook for 20-25 minutes.

Remove the pan from the heat and allow to cool slightly before transferring to a blender. Puree using all the cooking liquid.

Transfer the pureed mixture back into the pan and place over medium heat. When it begins to bubble, add the salt, sugar and cornmeal. Stir and cook over a low heat for 15-20 minutes or until the excess moisture evaporates.

Make the sauce: In a small pan over medium heat, heat the ghee or butter, add the ginger strips and chili powder and stir. Pour the spiced butter over the greens, removing the ginger strips before serving.

Submitted by: Kelly Gibbens, The Kansas City Star

Favorite thing about this recipe: Mustard greens are usually associated with Southern cooking but in India they are often used and along with the burst of ginger this is an unexpected ingredient.

Zucchini with Walnuts and Roquefort

- 3 medium zucchini, sliced thin
- 3 Tbsp walnut oil
- 2 tsp aged balsamic vinegar
- 1/2 tsp freshly grated black pepper
- 2 oz Roquefort cheese
- 1/4 cup walnuts, coarsely chopped

Total time: 10 minutes
Serves 4

Place a steamer rack over a pot of boiling water, add zucchini slices. Cover and steam until tender, about 3 minutes.

Transfer the zucchini slices to a bowl, pour the walnut oil and vinegar over and sprinkle with pepper. Crumble the cheese over the warm zucchini and turn the slices. Add 1/2 of the walnuts and turn again. Sprinkle with the remaining walnuts and serve.

Submitted by: Kelly Gibbens, The Kansas City Star

Favorite thing about this recipe: Walnut oil is a wonderful oil that in my opinion is often overlooked and can add so much flavor to a simple recipe.

Ruth's Cheeseball

- 3 Tbsp butter, softened
- 8 oz cream cheese, softened
- 1/4 tsp hot sauce
- 1/2 tsp Worcestershire sauce
- 1/3 cup green olives, chopped
- 1/4 cup black olives, chopped
- 1 Tbsp onion, grated
- 1/2 cup cheddar cheese, grated
- 1/3 cup parsley, chopped
- Cherry tomatoes (for serving)

Total time: 1 hour, 20 minutes
Serves 6-8

Cream butter, cream cheese, hot sauce and Worcestershire sauce together. Add olives, onion and cheddar cheese. Form into a ball, chill until set (about 1 hour). When ready to serve, roll in chopped parsley. Nice to serve around the holidays; make a ring around the bottom with cherry tomatoes if desired. Serve with crackers.

Submitted by: Joie Austin, The Herald-Sun

Favorite thing about this recipe: My grandma got this recipe from her neighbor Ruth years ago. It is a staple on every holiday table for my family!

Cumin Carrot Salad

- 1/2 lb carrots (about 4 medium), peeled and ends trimmed
- 1 1/4 Tbsp water
- Chicken broth
- 2 Tbsp white wine or Champagne vinegar
- 1 large clove garlic, mashed to a paste
- 1/4 tsp dried ground cumin, plus more to taste
- 1/4 tsp dried oregano
- 1/4 tsp sweet Spanish paprika
- Salt

Total time: 6 hours, 30 minutes
Serves 4

In a saucepan, place the carrots with a mixture of water and chicken broth, just enough to cover. (I usually add an equal amount of each.) Simmer for about 10 minutes, depending on the thickness of the carrots, until just about done but still slightly crisp.

Cool and cut into 1/2 -inch slices.

In a small bowl, mix together the vinegar, water, garlic, cumin, oregano, paprika and salt. Fold gently into the carrots. Marinate for several hours or overnight.

Submitted by: Kelly Gibbens, The Kansas City Star

Favorite thing about this recipe: The combination of cumin and Spanish paprika reminds me of so many meals when I was living in Spain.

Waldorf Salad

- 6 cups apples, chopped
- 1 cup celery, chopped
- 1 cup walnuts, chopped
- 1 cup grapes, halved
- 1 cup mayonnaise
- 1/2 cup raisins

Total time: 1 hour
Serves 20

Mix all ingredients together and chill.

Submitted by: Jessie Kirkbride, The Kansas City Star

Favorite thing about this recipe: Simple and delicious.

Kelly Mustard Gibbens

- 4 cups red potatoes, unpeeled and cubed
- 2 cups baby carrots
- 1 large red onion, sliced into 1/4-inch strips
- 1 Tbsp balsamic vinegar
- 4-5 tsp extra-virgin olive oil
- 1 clove garlic, minced
- 1 tsp dried thyme
- 1 tsp rosemary, crushed
- 1 tsp sage, rubbed
- 1 cup green beans, sliced
- 1/4 tsp kosher salt
- 1/2 tsp ground black pepper

Total time: 55-60 minutes
Serves 6

Heat the oven to 400 F.

Toss the prepared vegetables, except the green beans, along with the balsamic vinegar, olive oil, garlic and herbs. Arrange the vegetables in a lightly oiled large roasting pan. Roast the vegetables for 35 minutes, stirring every 10 minutes.

Add the sliced green beans to the pan and roast the vegetables for an additional 10 minutes. Arrange the roasted vegetables on the serving platter and season with salt and pepper.

Submitted by: Kelly Gibbens, The Kansas City Star

Favorite thing about this recipe: This is one of my favorite recipes as I can break out my aged balsamic vinegar with its luscious syrupy consistency.

Outta Sight Stuffed Celery

photo on page 95

- 1 bunch celery
- 1/2 cup red onion, finely chopped
- 8-oz package cream cheese, softened
- 2 tsp milk
- 1/4 tsp salt
- 1/2 tsp black pepper
- Paprika for decoration

Total time: 30 minutes
Serves 5-8

Wash, trim and shave celery — please don't skip this step. You don't want people walking around with celery strings stuck between their teeth.

Keep leaves on several small and tender stalks for decoration. The ones on the inside, close to the core, are good for this.

Cut celery into approximately 4-inch pieces lengthwise, although different lengths are fine. Pat dry.

Using a fork, mix the softened cream cheese, onion, milk, salt and pepper together. You want a smooth consistency, not runny. You may add a little more milk if necessary.

Scoop mixture onto each piece of celery. Arrange on a pretty glass plate or dish. Sprinkle lightly with paprika.

You will have some celery left over, which is a good reason to double the recipe!

You may prepare the celery and cream cheese mixture a day ahead of time. Be sure to store them separately.

Stuff the celery shortly before time to serve.

Submitted by: Renee McCormick, The Kansas City Star

Favorite thing about this recipe: My favorite thing about this recipe is it's fast, easy and absolutely delicious. Everybody always raves over it, and they ask for the recipe. I love to serve stuffed celery for Thanksgiving and Christmas. It really jazzes up my holiday table.

Collard Green and Olive Pesto Pasta Salad

- 1 cup Kalamata olives, pitted
- 2 large cloves garlic, whole and peeled
- 1 lb collard greens, washed, trimmed and chopped
- 2 Tbsp fresh lemon juice
- 1 tsp lemon zest
- 1 Tbsp Champagne or white wine vinegar
- 1 tsp kosher salt
- 1 tsp freshly ground black pepper
- 1 cup extra-virgin olive oil
- 1 cup Parmesan cheese, grated, plus additional for topping
- 8 oz rotini pasta
- 1 cup grape tomatoes, halved

Total time: 50-60 minutes
Serves 4

In a food processor, pulse the olives and garlic cloves until finely chopped. Add the collard greens, lemon juice and zest, vinegar, salt and pepper, pulse until the collard greens are finely chopped.

With the processor running, pour the olive oil through the food chute in a slow and steady stream. Once it is completely incorporated, add the grated Parmesan cheese and pulse until smooth. Keep in an airtight container in the refrigerator until ready to use.

Bring a large pot of salted water to a boil and cook the pasta to al dente as per the package directions. Once cooked, drain the pasta.

Combine the dressing and pasta, and refrigerate until all the ingredients are properly chilled.

Just before serving, drizzle with additional olive oil, grape tomatoes and additional grated Parmesan cheese.

Submitted by: Kelly Gibbens, The Kansas City Star

Favorite thing about this recipe: The collard greens make for a surprising addition to a pasta salad.

Roast Cauliflower

- 1 large head cauliflower
- 4 Tbsp butter, melted and divided
- Kosher salt
- Freshly ground black pepper
- 4 whole cloves garlic (skin-on)
- 4 leaves fresh sage
- 4 sprigs fresh thyme
- 4 sprigs fresh rosemary
- 4 sprigs fresh oregano

Total time: 1 hour, 30 minutes
Serves 4

Heat oven to 450 F.

In a large oven-safe skillet, place cauliflower, rub all over with 2 Tbsp of melted butter and season with salt and pepper. Arrange garlic and herbs around cauliflower.

Bake 1 hour to 1 hour 30 minutes, until cauliflower is tender and slightly charred. Brush with remaining 2 Tbsp melted butter halfway through. (Pierce cauliflower with a paring knife to check if it's ready.)

Submitted by: Thomas Arnhold, The Kansas City Star

Favorite thing about this recipe: The simplicity and ease of preparation.

Maple Bacon Carrots

- 12 medium carrots, peeled
- 12 strips bacon
- 1/4 cup maple syrup
- Brown sugar
- Freshly ground black pepper

Total time: 35 minutes
Serves 12

Heat oven to 400 F or start grill.

Wrap each carrot in one strip of bacon, and place bacon ends down on a large baking sheet. Brush all over with maple syrup and season with black pepper.

Bake or grill 10 minutes, remove from oven or grill, and brush with remaining maple syrup and dust with brown sugar. You may want to turn the carrots as well.

Bake or grill 15 minutes more, or until carrots are tender and bacon is crisp. Serve.

Submitted by: Thomas Arnhold, The Kansas City Star

Favorite thing about this recipe: You can make it in the oven or on the grill!

Stuffed Pumpkin

- Small pie pumpkin (sugar pumpkin)
- 1 lb Italian sausage
- 1/2 onion, sliced
- 1 small zucchini sliced
- 1 box cornbread stuffing

Total time: 1 hour, 30 minutes
Serves 6

Heat oven to 350 F.

Cut top off (save it for later) pumpkin and clean out the insides.

Brown sausage with onion and zucchini.

Make cornbread stuffing as directed by package.

Combine sausage with stuffing and stuff into pumpkin.

Put top on pumpkin and set it in a baking dish. Add water half full in the baking dish. Bake for 1 hour or until pumpkin shell is done.

Put on serving plate and slice into 6 pieces. Eat with a spoon to get a piece of pumpkin in each bite.

Submitted by: Elizabeth McKie, The Kansas City Star

Favorite thing about this recipe: An excellent use of pumpkin as a vegetable.

Corn and Cheese Casserole

- 16-oz can cream style corn
- 16-oz can whole kernel corn drained
- 8.5-oz box corn muffin mix
- 1 cup sour cream
- 1/2 cup butter or margarine, melted
- 6 oz cheese, grated

Total time: 1 hour, 20 minutes
Serves 8-10

Heat oven to 350 F.

Mix all ingredients except cheese and pour into a greased 13x9 casserole dish.

Top with grated cheese, bake for about 40-50 minutes. If you'd like this spiced up, add 4.5-oz can chopped green chilies.

Submitted by: Lynell Caldsell, The Kansas City Star

Favorite thing about this recipe: Easy to prepare and quick.

EZ-PZ Stuffed Mushrooms

- 8 oz white button mushrooms, stems removed and saved
- 3-4 green onions, finely chopped (include green and white parts)
- 1 Tbsp extra-virgin olive oil (good grade)
- 1 Tbsp unsalted butter
- 1/2 cup cheese pieces, cut small (any kind of cheese such as cheddar, Gruyere, Monterey Jack, Colby)
- Salt and pepper to taste
- A pinch of smoked paprika (optional)

Total time: 30 minutes
Serves 6

Heat oven to 350 F and place oven rack in middle position.

Wipe mushrooms clean with damp paper towel. Place hole side up on sheet pan.

Mince mushroom stems finely and mix with finely chopped green onions.

In saute pan over medium heat, melt olive oil and butter. Add onion mixture and saute until soft and fragrant. Place cheese pieces down in hole of mushrooms (2-3 is usually enough).

Spoon onion mixture over mushrooms with small spoon pushing gently until mixture meets cheese pieces nicely.

Bake for 12-15 minutes. Serve hot or room temperature.

Submitted by: Sandra Scott, Lexington Herald-Leader

Favorite thing about this recipe: It's easy and can be changed by adding or taking away.

Sauteed Cheese

- 1 Tbsp olive oil
- 1 clove garlic, minced
- 4 oz mozzarella cheese, grated
- 1 oz Parmesan cheese, grated

Total time: 15 minutes
Serves 2

Liberally coat a nonstick frying pan with olive oil. Spread mozzarella in the bottom. Scatter the garlic in. Cover with Parmesan. Fry medium-low until all cheese melts and turns golden brown on bottom.

Submitted by: Danny Brumfield, Lexington Herald-Leader

Favorite thing about this recipe: Best part of pizza sans other junk.

Granny Pat's Mashed Potatoes

photo on page 99

- 4-5 large russet potatoes
- 1/2 cup, plus 4 Tbsp salted butter
- 2 celery stalks, diced
- 1 small onion, diced
- 1-2 Tbsp sour cream
- 1/4 cup half-and-half
- Salt and pepper

Total time: 45 minutes
Serves 8-12

Peel and cube potatoes. Place in saucepan and cover with water. Turn temperature to medium-high to cook. Add 1 tsp salt. Cover with lid and cook the potatoes until they are very tender.

While potatoes cook, place diced onion and celery in 2 Tbsp butter and saute 3-4 minutes until onions are translucent. Stir often.

When potatoes are tender, strain water from the pan. Use a handheld potato masher and mash the potatoes until they are completely free of lumps. Add one stick of softened butter to the hot potatoes and continue blending until the butter has melted. Give the potatoes a taste test to see how much salt and pepper is needed.

Add sour cream to potatoes. Heat half-and-half. Reserve 1 Tbsp, and add to the potatoes a little at a time until they are the consistency you want, not too thin.

Add sauteed onion and celery. While potatoes are hot, place them in a casserole dish. Smooth out the top of the potatoes and pour remaining 1 Tbsp of the hot half-and-half over the potatoes to keep them fluffy. Press the back of a large spoon in the center of the potatoes to make a dip then place a large pat of butter (remaining 2 Tbsp) in the dip to melt.

A holiday meal is not complete without a hot dish of buttery mashed potatoes.

Leftovers are great for making potato cakes. Just mix with a little flour and pat out the patties in a skillet of hot oil.

Submitted by: Patricia O'Neal, Lexington Herald-Leader

Favorite thing about this recipe: It's delicious and everybody loves mashed potatoes.

Dress for the Occasion Pasta

- 12-oz package of bow tie pasta
- 3 Tbsp vegetable oil
- 1 yellow onion, chopped
- 3 cloves garlic, sliced
- 28-oz can diced tomatoes
- Salt and pepper
- 1 lb Jack cheese

Total time: 1 hour
Serves 6-8

In a large pot, boil pasta in six cups of water until al dente. Drain and place pasta in large baking dish.

In a skillet over low heat, saute chopped yellow onion and sliced garlic in vegetable oil, until onion is translucent.

Add diced tomatoes and stir. Add salt and pepper to taste. Place lid on pot. Simmer 20 minutes.

Heat oven to 350 F.

Place tomato saute in baking dish with pasta. Stir together.

Add shredded cheese. Mix well. Place lid on baking dish. Bake 35 minutes.

Submitted by: Carol Melgosa, Merced Sun-Star

Favorite thing about this recipe: My blessing food, comforts the soul for family and friends.

Festive Zucchini Medley

- 1 onion, diced
- 4 cloves garlic, sliced
- 2 Tbsp vegetable oil
- 2 zucchini, sliced into 1/4-inch rounds then quartered
- 2 yellow crookneck squash, sliced into 1/4-inch rounds then quartered
- 14.5-oz can sweet corn
- 14.5-oz can diced tomatoes, drained
- 1 tsp salt
- 1/2 tsp pepper
- 1 lb Jack cheese, grated

Total time: 1 hour
Serves 6-8

Heat oven to 350 F.

In a large pot, add vegetable oil and saute onion and garlic until translucent. Add zucchini and yellow squash. Stir and cook for 10 minutes, or until zucchini and squash begin to get soft (when pierced by fork).

Add corn, including liquid. Add diced tomatoes that have been drained. Add salt and pepper and taste for flavor. Add grated cheese and mix until blended.

Place zucchini medley in a greased baking dish. Bake for 35 minutes.

Submitted by: Carol Melgosa, Merced Sun-Star

Favorite thing about this recipe: This festive dish is delicious and colorful. The medley of colors make a beautiful celebration to any occasion.

Celebration Zucchini Delightfully Stuffed

- 5 large zucchini, sliced lengthwise
- 10 cups water
- Button mushrooms, chopped
- 4 Tbsp butter, melted
- 1 Tbsp flour
- 1 tsp oregano
- 1 cup sour cream
- 1 cup Jack cheese, grated
- 1 cup Parmesan cheese, grated

Total time: 1 hour, 15 minutes
Serves 6-8

In a large pot, bring 10 cups water and zucchini to medium boil. Cook zucchini until al dente, when pierced with fork. Remove zucchini from water and place on greased 9x13 baking dish. Let cool.

With spoon, remove the center of each zucchini making each one hollowed like a "boat."

Heat oven to 350 F.

In a saucepan, saute butter and chopped button mushrooms, cook 10-15 minutes. Add flour and oregano. Mix thoroughly. Remove from heat.

Add sour cream and Jack cheese. Stir until completely combined. With a spoon, place cheese mixture inside each zucchini boat.

Bake for 35 minutes. Sprinkle Parmesan cheese onto the top of each baked zucchini boat and broil for 2 minutes. Careful not to over broil.

Submitted by: Carol Melgosa, Merced Sun-Star

Favorite thing about this recipe: Very delicious and when displayed on special serving dish, will be a festive dish for your meal.

Portuguese Beans Divino

- 8 cups water
- 16-oz package dry pinto beans
- 8-oz can tomato sauce
- 2 Tbsp cinnamon
- 1 tsp salt
- 1 lb bacon, cut in 1-inch pieces
- 1 lb Portuguese linguica, sliced and cooked (optional)

**Total time: 3 hours to 3 hours, 30 minutes
Serves 6-8**

In a large pot with water, place pinto beans (sort through beans and remove dried pieces), tomato sauce, cinnamon and salt, simmer on low.

In a frying pan, cook bacon stirring continuously until cooked. Remove bacon from frying pan and place in the beans and water. Cover with lid.

Cook on low heat for 2-3 hours. Sauce should thicken. Stir occasionally, as needed.

Submitted by: Mary Correia Hatfield, Merced Sun-Star

Favorite thing about this recipe:
Portuguese beans are a staple food in large families. These beans have been served in the Correia family for 70 years. Mom is now 81 years and still cooks regularly.

Watermelon Salad

- Watermelon
- Crumbled feta cheese
- Cilantro
- Balsamic vinegar (optional)

**Total time: 5 minutes
Serves 1 or more**

Cut chilled watermelon into bite-size cubes and place in a bowl. Add crumbled feta cheese. Toss together with chopped cilantro. Add a little balsamic vinegar to individual plates to taste.

Submitted by: Jan Novar, Miami Herald

Favorite thing about this recipe: A refreshing salad with minimal prep time. Ease and unusual flavors of three items combined.

Sweet Corn Pudding

- 4 cups corn kernels (about 19 oz frozen) or 5 ears (fresh)
- 4 Tbsp butter, room temperature
- 4 large eggs
- 1 cup half-and-half
- 1/2 cup whole milk
- 4 Tbsp sugar
- 2 Tbsp all-purpose flour
- 2 tsp baking powder
- 1 tsp salt

Total time: 1 hour, 25 minutes
Serves 8

Heat oven to 350 F.

Thaw corn if using frozen. If fresh, shave off the cob.

Butter an 8x8-inch glass baking dish.

Set aside about one-third of the corn (about 1 1/3 cups). Blend the rest of the ingredients in food processor until almost smooth.

Stir in reserved corn and pour batter into prepared dish. Bake until brown and center is just set, about 45-55 minutes.

Cool 10 minutes; serve.

Tip: make this in the morning and warm in a low oven. It's better after it sits awhile.

Submitted by: Teresa Carr, Miami Herald

Favorite thing about this recipe: It's easy, very tasty and a great fall dish.

Zucchini Souffle

- 2 medium zucchini
- 3 Tbsp vinegar
- 2 eggs
- 2 Tbsp wheat flour
- 2 Tbsp corn flour
- 1 tsp baking powder
- 1 tsp salt
- 1 tsp Badia Sazón Tropical seasoning blend
- 1 Tbsp Parmesan cheese

Total time: 1 hour, 20 minutes
Serves 8

Heat oven to 370 F.

Peel and grate zucchini; put it in a bowl with 3 cups water and vinegar. After 20 minutes, drain and squeeze zucchini to remove water.

In a bowl, beat the eggs, add the wheat and corn flours, baking powder, salt, seasonings, Parmesan cheese and drained zucchini. Mix all the ingredients.

Prepare baking pan with cooking spray; add mixture and bake for approximately 30 minutes.

Submitted by: Susana Menda, Miami Herald

Favorite thing about this recipe: It's for those who don't want to gain weight!

Tuscan Picnic Sardine Pie

photo on page 100

Batter

- 2 cups milk
- 4 eggs
- 11 Tbsp all-purpose flour
- 10 Tbsp olive oil
- 3 oz Parmesan cheese, grated
- 1 Tbsp baking powder

Filling

- Two 7.5-oz tins sardines in tomato sauce, chopped (such as Crown Prince brand)
- 30 black olives

Total time: 1 hour
Serves 8

Heat oven to 350 F.

In a blender, combine all batter ingredients and mix well.

Pour 1/2 the batter into a greased 11x8-inch baking dish.

Top with the chopped sardines and evenly spread the olives. Cover with the remainder of the batter. Bake for approximately 45 minutes.

Submitted by: Fernanda Teixeira, Miami Herald

Favorite thing about this recipe: Easy to serve at picnics, economical and delicious.

Double Cornbread

- 2 large eggs
- 2 cups buttermilk (or soured milk*)
- 1/2 cup melted butter or oil
- 2 cups cornmeal
- 2 cups whole wheat flour
- 1/4 cup sugar
- 4 tsp baking powder
- 1 tsp baking soda
- 1/2 tsp salt
- 1/2 cup canned corn, drained

Total time: 35-40 minutes
Serves 20-24

*Soured Milk
Measure out milk and add 1 Tbsp vinegar or lemon juice for each cup of milk. Let sit 5-10 minutes to clabber.

Heat oven to 425 F.

Crack eggs into buttermilk and whisk well to blend.

Place butter or oil in 9x13 pan. When oven is heated, place pan in oven to melt butter (or heat the oil slightly) about 20-30 seconds.

Remove pan from oven, sprinkle in 1/2 the dry ingredients, drained corn and the liquids. Whisk vigorously to blend and then add rest of the dry ingredients while continuing to whisk. Smooth top when fully blended.

Bake for 20-25 minutes. Cool for 10 minutes before serving.

Submitted by: Louise Sugiyama, The Modesto Bee

Favorite thing about this recipe: Variation on my Mom's old recipe with added nutrition from the whole wheat and corn.

Salmon Raisin Spread

photo on page 95
- 2/3 cup mayonnaise
- 1 tsp curry powder
- 3 green onions, finely chopped
- 2 Tbsp mixed raisins, finely chopped
- 1 celery stalk, finely chopped
- 1 cup smoked salmon, crumbled
- Crackers

Total time: 15 minutes
Serves 2 or more

Mix together mayonnaise and curry powder. Stir in green onions, raisins and celery. Add salmon and gently blend together. Serve with crackers.

Submitted by: Karen Sodhi, The Olympian

Favorite thing about this recipe: Mixed raisins add a great taste to the smoked salmon.

Sausage Cabbage

- 2 cups purple cabbage, shredded
- 2 cups green cabbage, shredded
- 2 Tbsp olive oil
- 1/2 medium green pepper, sliced
- 1/2 medium red onion, sliced
- 1 tsp garlic, minced
- 1 lb Hillshire Farm Smoked Sausage, sliced
- 1/2 tsp salt
- 1/2 tsp black pepper
- 1/4 tsp Slap Ya Mama Cajun Seasoning
- 1/2 cup zesty Italian dressing

Total time: 1 hour
Serves 12

Wash and drain cabbage.

In a stock pot, heat olive oil on medium. Add green pepper, onion, garlic and sausage. Then add cabbage and stir. Let simmer for about 10 minutes. Add 1/4 cup of water. Add salt, pepper and seasoning, stir. Add Italian dressing. Turn heat to low and simmer for 15 more minutes and turn off heat. Serve.

Submitted by: Deborah Thompson, The Rock Hill Herald

Favorite thing about this recipe: Quick and easy.

Decadent Mac and Cheese

- 4 Tbsp unsalted butter
- 1/2 cup flour
- 3 cups chicken stock
- 2 cups heavy cream
- 2 tsp white or black pepper
- 1 1/2 tsp kosher or regular salt
- 1/4 tsp paprika
- 1 1/4 lb medium cheddar cheese, grated
- 1 1/4 lb sharp cheddar cheese, grated
- 7 cups cooked pasta

Total time: 1 hour
Serves 8-10

Heat oven to 350 F.

Melt butter. Add flour to form roux; stir until flour and butter are mixed. Slowly add chicken stock. Slowly add heavy cream. Add spices. Add cheeses small amounts at a time; mix until melted. Fold sauce into pasta in a lightly buttered pan.

Put in oven 35-45 minutes until the mac and cheese gets lightly brown. If you like your mac and cheese to have a kick, add a little bit of Gorgonzola.

Submitted by: Steven Berkowitz, The Herald-Sun

Favorite thing about this recipe: The best mac and cheese I have ever had!

Okra a la Maria

- 2 large packages frozen okra
- Salt
- Wine vinegar (red or white)
- Olive oil
- 14.5-oz can diced tomatoes
- 2-3 cloves of garlic, minced
- Black pepper

Total time: 3 hours
Serves 8-10

Put the frozen okra in a stainless steel bowl. Add salt to taste and vinegar to taste. Be generous with the vinegar. Place the bowl in the refrigerator overnight (preferable) or for 2-3 hours.

Heat oven to 350 F.

Brush a clay pan with oil — it is not as good in glass dishes. Add the bowl of okra, including the salt and vinegar, to the pan. Add the tomatoes and stir a little. Add garlic and stir again to mix well. Add pepper if you wish, and then add olive oil. Be generous — at least 1/2 cup.

Bake for at least 2 1/2 hours. Bon appetit!

Notes

Sometimes I add cut potatoes among the okra. Other times, I cut a whole chicken along the breastbone and during the last hour and a half of baking the okra I salt and pepper the chicken and lay it down over the okra basting it with the "sauce" of the okra. Thus, one has a complete meal. Meat/vegetable or meat/potatoes/vegetable.

You can use fresh okra but make sure you do not cut the stems off. You do not want to expose the inside of the okra. Peel the stems with a sharp knife all around so you end up with a little pyramid-shaped cone.

It freezes very well and also tastes better the next day as leftovers.

My mother in Greece cooked this dish very differently, but all my Greek friends love my simplified version. My American friends who did not like okra before (too slimy) love this dish, which is not at all slimy and has a wonderful flavor.

Submitted by: Maria Contou Christopher, The Herald-Sun

Favorite thing about this recipe: It reminds me of my mother's cooking in Athens, Greece.

Tastin' Jamaican Shark Bites Salad

photo on page 102

- 1 1/2 lb blacktip shark (or other firm, white fish)
- Tastin' Jamaican Caribbean Jerk (TastinJamaican.com) or Cajun Style Seasoning
- Romaine and iceberg lettuces
- Fresh spinach leaves
- Red cabbage
- Red onion, thinly sliced
- Sugar snap peas
- Tomatoes
- Cucumber
- Yellow bell pepper
- Carrots
- Fresh broccoli florets
- Salad toppings such as honey-roasted pecans and sunflower seeds
- Sun-dried tomato vinaigrette dressing
- Tastin' Jamaican Cranberry Salsa (TastinJamaican.com)

Total time: 20 minutes
Serves 6

Note

It's best to soak shark meat overnight in an acidic liquid like orange juice to get rid of any strong taste.

After soaking, cut shark meat into 1-inch cubes. Coat with seasoning and sear until cooked through.

Prepare salad ingredients.

Add shark bites to individual salad servings, drizzle with dressing, add toppings, and garnish with several spoonfuls of Tastin' Jamaican Cranberry Salsa.

Submitted by: Melissa Hodges, The News & Observer (Raleigh)

Favorite thing about this recipe: When fishing nets you a shark, keep it and use this recipe! If you don't have shark meat, any firm fish will do. Simple, yet a nutritious way to make your day of fishing a success!

Nanny's Challah Bread

photo on page 98

- 2 packets Fleischmann's Active Dry Yeast
- 2 cups very warm water
- 1/2 cup sugar
- 9 cups white flour
- 2 tsp salt
- 4 large eggs (reserve 1 for egg wash)
- 1/3 cup vegetable oil
- 2 Tbsp honey
- Poppy seeds

Total time: 6 hours, 30 minutes
Yields 2 large loaves or 4 small loaves

In small bowl, mix yeast with warm water and 1/4 cup sugar and set aside.

Combine dry ingredients. Add 3 eggs, oil, honey and yeast. Knead 10 minutes by hand or 2-3 minutes with stand mixer.

Let it rise 2 hours (until doubled). Punch down.

Knead briefly and let it rise again for 2 hours. When risen, braid it on a baking pan sprayed with cooking spray. Can be made into 2 large loaves or 4 smaller ones.

Let it rise, keeping an eye that it doesn't over-rise and start to spread.

Heat oven to 350 F.

Brush with beaten egg. Sprinkle with poppy seeds. Bake in a greased pan for 25 minutes.

Submitted by: Barbara Silver,
The Herald-Sun

Favorite thing about this recipe: All my friends and family exclaim it's the best challah they've ever had.

Turkey Stuffing

photo on page 101

- 1 Tbsp sugar
- 1/2 cup raisins
- 1/4 cup orange juice
- 1 Tbsp butter or margarine, plus more for top
- 1/2 cup apple, chopped
- 1 cup croutons
- 7-oz package long grain and wild rice blend

Total time: 30 minutes
Serves 6-8

Heat oven to 350 F.

In saucepan, combine sugar, raisins, orange juice and butter. Cook, stirring, over low heat until the butter melts and mixture is heated through.

Add the chopped apple and cook another 2 minutes, then add the croutons. Stir the mixture until all of the liquid is absorbed. Remove from heat.

Prepare rice according to package directions and add to orange juice mixture.

Stuff turkey, if desired, or transfer stuffing to a baking dish, dot with butter and bake until heated through.

Serve with roast chicken, turkey or other poultry. This recipe can be doubled and tripled.

Submitted by: Lauren Watral, The News & Observer (Raleigh)

Favorite thing about this recipe: The tradition — it has a story as to why I created it, which we share every year at Thanksgiving!

Zucchini and Carrots with Pancetta

photo on page 103

- 1/4 lb thin-sliced pancetta
- Shallot, sliced thinly
- 2 cloves garlic, sliced thinly
- 3 large carrots, cut into matchsticks
- 1/2 cup low-sodium chicken stock
- 2 zucchini, cut into 1-inch pieces

Total time: 45 minutes
Serves 6-8

With scissors, cut the pancetta into 1-inch square pieces.

In a large skillet over medium-high heat, cook pancetta with 1/4 cup water. Cook until the water is evaporated and turn down the heat to medium. Fry until the pancetta has browned. Remove the pancetta with a slotted spoon and place it on a paper towel lined plate to cool. Save pan with drippings.

In same pan, fry the thinly sliced shallot over medium heat until soft. Add the garlic and cook for 30 seconds. Stir frequently. Add the carrots to the pan along with the chicken stock and salt, raising the heat to medium high. Cook until the chicken stock has just evaporated. Add the zucchini and cook until the zucchini is tender-crisp, stirring frequently.

Sprinkle the cooked pancetta over the top of the vegetables.

Submitted by: Nicholas Verna, The News & Observer (Raleigh)

Favorite thing about this recipe: Using the oil from the pancetta in place of olive oil gives this dish a spicy decadence that you rarely find in vegetables.

Julie's Apple Butter

photo on page 99

- 12 cooking apples: peeled, cored and sliced
- 2 1/4 cup sugar
- 2 tsp cinnamon
- 1/2 tsp ground cloves
- 1/2 tsp allspice
- 2 Tbsp honey
- 1/2 tsp vanilla
- 1/4 tsp orange extract
- 1 Tbsp light brown sugar
- 2 1/2 Tbsp applesauce
- 1 1/4 cup apple cider
- A pinch of nutmeg

Total time: 7 hours, 40 minutes
Yields 4 1/3 cups

Combine all ingredients in a slow cooker on high for 4 hours. Stir and then cook on high for 2 more hours. Cool for 1 hour.

Puree all but 1/3 cup in a blender. Mix the 1/3 cup remaining chunky apple butter into the pureed apple butter at the end.

Put in containers and store up to 3 weeks in the refrigerator. Spread the apple butter on some fluffy, warm biscuits and enjoy!

Submitted by: Julie Pechanek, The Charlotte Observer

Favorite thing about this recipe: Apple butter on biscuits is one of my favorite fall things! Blue skies, chilly air, leaves falling and the smell of apples and spices in the slow cooker for hours. Perfect way to start the fall season!

Holiday Slaw

Salad

- 1 red apple, thinly sliced
- 1 green apple, thinly sliced
- 14-oz bag coleslaw mix
- 2 green onions, sliced

Dressing

- 1/3 cup real mayonnaise
- 3 Tbsp honey
- 2 Tbsp sour cream

Total time: 15 minutes
Serves 6

Combine dressing ingredients and mix with salad. Serve immediately.

Submitted by: Jennifer Anderson, The Wichita Eagle

Favorite thing about this recipe: Sweet and tangy.

My Cornbread Stuffing

- 1 lb hot breakfast sausage
- 1 Tbsp butter
- 1 onion, chopped
- 4 celery stalks, chopped
- 2 cloves garlic, minced
- 1/2-1 cup corn (frozen, fresh or canned)
- 12-oz bag cornbread stuffing
- 2-3 cups chicken stock

Total time: 50 minutes
Serves 8

Heat oven to 350 F.

Cook sausage until very little red left. Drain some oil. How much will depend on the brand you buy — leave a small amount in pan.

Add butter, onions, celery and continue cooking until soft and sausage is nicely browned.

Add garlic and cook for 2 more minutes, until you can smell the garlic.

Add the corn and the cornbread stuffing and stir to combine. Then add about 2 cups of the chicken stock and mix until uniformly moistened. Add more as needed to make all the dressing moist.

Place in a 9x9 baking dish and leave the top craggy so it will brown with lots of crunchy parts.

Bake uncovered for about 30 minutes until the top is crispy.

Submitted by: Nelson J. Mendoza, The News & Observer (Raleigh)

Favorite thing about this recipe:
Great savory flavor.

Smoked Chicken Spread

- 3 cups cooked chicken, shredded
- 3/4 cup mayonnaise
- 1/3 cup sweet pickle relish
- 1/4 cup celery, finely chopped
- 1 tsp Dijon mustard
- 1/4-1/2 tsp salt (optional or to taste)
- 1/4 tsp black pepper
- 1/2 tsp liquid smoke

Total time: 30 minutes
Serves 3-4

Mix all ingredients together.

Serve cold with crackers as a spread, as a sandwich or in a salad.

Submitted by: Karen Thomas, The Sacramento Bee

Favorite thing about this recipe: Easy and tasty.

Betty's Beans

- 1 lb Jimmy Dean sausage, original
- 1 lb Jimmy Dean sausage, hot
- 2 cups onion, chopped
- 2 cups celery, sliced
- 1 can tomato paste
- 1 can Campbell's Tomato Soup
- 1 cup brown sugar
- 2 cans wax string beans, drained
- 2 cans green beans, drained
- 1 large can pork and beans
- 1 can red kidney beans, drained
- 1 can hot chili beans

Total time: 1 hour, 20 minutes
Serves 8-10

Heat oven to 350 F.

Saute sausage with the onion and celery. Add tomato paste, soup and brown sugar. Stir in the remaining ingredients.

Bake 1 hour.

Submitted by: Anastasia Hjelle, The Sacramento Bee

Favorite thing about this recipe: Not just a boring side dish, it's hearty and flavorful!

Best Dilled Potato Salad

- 8 lbs russet potatoes, scrubbed and halved but not peeled*
- Salted water to cover
- 4 eggs, hard-boiled, shelled and chopped
- 3/4 cup green onions, finely chopped including tops
- 3/4 cup celery, minced
- 3 Tbsp Dijon mustard
- 4 Tbsp dill relish (or 1 dill pickle, chopped, and 2 Tbsp pickle juice)
- 1 Tbsp dried dill weed
- 1 Tbsp dried basil
- 1/2 tsp garlic powder
- Salt and pepper to taste
- 2 cups real mayonnaise

*Important
Peeling and cubing the potatoes before cooking changes both the taste and the texture. Not recommended.

Total time: 1 hour, 30 minutes
Serves 16-18

Boil potatoes until easily pierced with a fork. Drain and cool, then peel and cube into bite-sized pieces. Place in large bowl.

In a separate bowl, combine remaining ingredients. Stir mixture into the potatoes, mixing well, and correct seasonings to taste.

Cover and place in refrigerator.

At serving time, stir once again and correct seasonings if needed. Sprinkle with paprika. Serves 16-18 hungry guests. Recipe can be halved for a smaller group.

Submitted by: Janet Comstock, The Sacramento Bee

Favorite thing about this recipe: This is a favorite at gatherings of friends and family. Leftovers are fought over and taken home.

Gourmet Restaurant-Style Mexican Rice

- 1 Tbsp olive oil
- 1/2 red onion, finely diced
- 1 tsp garlic, minced
- 6-oz can black olives in liquid
- 14.5-oz can diced tomatoes with green chiles
- 1 tsp coconut aminos
- 1 cup chicken broth
- 2 drops cilantro essential oil (or 1/4 cup fresh, chopped)
- 1/8 tsp cumin
- 1/8 tsp smoked paprika
- 2 cups jasmine rice
- 1 small lime

Total time: 30 minutes
Serves 10

Note

To get started you will need a large measuring cup that holds at least 4 cups of liquid. You can use a smaller cup, just be sure to keep track of the total liquid.

In medium or large saucepan, add oil and heat over medium-high heat. Add onions and garlic, stirring occasionally, until onions are starting to get translucent and soft.

While this is cooking feel free to start next step to save time. Open olives and tomatoes, and drain all liquid into measuring cup. This should yield about 2 cups of liquid. Add coconut aminos and spices to liquid. Add chicken broth to liquid until you have 3 cups total. Stir to mix in the spices.

Once onion is cooked, pour liquid into pan, add rice and stir with a rice spoon or spatula (nothing metal) scraping the bottom to incorporate the onions and garlic into the mixture. Reduce heat to medium. Pour drained tomatoes on top of rice and cover until just starting to boil. Gently stir in the tomatoes then cover and reduce heat to low simmer.

Let cook for about 20 minutes or until rice is soft. Remove from heat.

Squeeze fresh lime juice over rice and gently fluff before serving.

Submitted by: Steven Butler, The Sacramento Bee

Favorite thing about this recipe: Super easy clean-up with only 1 pan and a measuring cup. Also the only salt added comes from the juice so no extra salt needed.

Fancy Green Beans

photo on page 96

- 1/2 cup sherry cooking wine
- 1/2 tsp Worcestershire sauce
- 1/2 tsp sugar
- 1 tsp lemon pepper
- 2 tsp chicken bouillon granules or 1/2 a regular 1-cup bouillon cube
- 6 slices thick-cut black pepper bacon, chopped
- 1/2 lb mushrooms, sliced
- 1 small-to-medium onion, thinly sliced
- 3 cloves garlic, grated or minced
- 1 lbs green beans, cleaned and snapped
- 1 can sliced water chestnuts with liquid
- 1/4 tsp each salt and freshly ground pepper
- 1 red bell pepper, chopped

Total time: 1 hour
Serves 4-6

In a measuring cup, combine sherry cooking wine, Worcestershire sauce, sugar, lemon pepper and bouillon, and mix until bouillon is dissolved. Set aside.

In large skillet with a lid, cook bacon on medium-high heat, stirring frequently. Once bacon is crispy, remove to a bowl and set aside.

In same pan, add the sliced mushrooms stir once to coat in the bacon drippings, then spread into even layer on bottom of the pan leave alone for about 5 minutes to cook without disturbing. Allow them to get some color.

Once mushrooms are to desired wellness, add the onion, garlic and the green beans to the pan. Stir in water chestnuts with liquid and wine mixture. Cook 2-3 minutes. Taste and decide if it's best to add the additional salt and pepper.

Place lid on and cook on medium heat for about 15-20 minutes, until green beans are desired tenderness. Toss in the red bell pepper and heat through.

This can be cooked to be served later; bring it to a boil at this point and turn heat off completely and allow to cool. Simply reheat just prior to serving.

Submitted by: Mary Beth Aguilera, The Sacramento Bee

Favorite thing about this recipe: It reminds me of when Grandma used to make green bean casserole for Thanksgiving or Christmas when I was growing up.

Pumpkin Soup

photo on page 94

- Olive oil
- 1 large onion, diced
- Salt and pepper to taste
- 3 cloves garlic, diced
- 1/2 cup dry white wine
- 6 cups fresh pumpkin, cut into 1-inch cubes
- 4 cups chicken broth
- For garnish: heavy whipping cream and parsley; for added texture you can add toasted pumpkin seeds.

Total time: 45 minutes
Serves 6-8

In a Dutch oven, add olive oil, just enough to coat the bottom of the pot. Heat olive oil over a medium heat, add onions and about a teaspoon of salt; cook onions until soft, about 3-5 minutes.

Add garlic and white wine, cook about 2 minutes. Add pumpkin and chicken broth and cook until the pumpkin is fork tender about 15-20 minutes.

For a richer taste, oven roast the pumpkin until tender and then follow the remaining directions.

When the pumpkin is tender, set aside about 1/2 cup to use as garnish, if desired.

Working in batches, puree the soup in a blender. Garnish with cream, reserved pumpkin and parsley.

Submitted by: Brenda O'Donnell, The Sacramento Bee

Favorite thing about this recipe: It's easy to make and looks great.

Broccoli Supreme Casserole

photo on page 96

- Three 10-oz packages frozen broccoli florets
- 8 Tbsp, plus 6 Tbsp butter, divided
- 3 chicken bouillon cubes
- 4 Tbsp flour
- 2 cups milk
- 2/3 cup water
- 2/3 cup walnuts, coarsely chopped (optional)
- 5.3 oz Pepperidge Farm Herb-Seasoned Classic Stuffing

Total time: 45 minutes
Serves 6-8

Heat oven to 375 F.

Place frozen broccoli in microwave-safe bowl, add 1/2 cup water, cover and microwave on high for 4 minutes. Drain.

Coarsely chop florets and place broccoli in 9x11 butter-coated baking dish.

Melt 8 Tbsp butter over low heat. Remove from heat and add bouillon cubes. Crush bouillon cubes once softened with spoon and blend thoroughly.

Add flour to butter mixture and blend. Make a roux by gradually adding milk to butter mixture, cooking over low heat and stirring constantly until thick and bubbly.

Pour milk mixture (roux) over broccoli and blend together.

Heat water until boiling, and add remaining butter. Add stuffing mix and walnuts. Blend together and sprinkle on top of broccoli.

Bake 30 minutes until bubbly and stuffing is lightly browned.

Submitted by: Dottie Mattioli, The Sacramento Bee

Favorite thing about this recipe: Versatility; pairs well with poultry and meats.

Farro with Spring Vegetables and Creme Fraiche

photo on page 98

- 8 cups water
- 1/2 cup apple cider vinegar
- Salt
- 1 cup farro
- 1/2 cup asparagus or snap peas, cut into bite-size pieces
- 1 Tbsp olive oil
- 1/4 cup creme fraiche
- Lemon juice
- 1 Tbsp fresh dill

Notes

You are cooking the farro "pasta style," meaning it is cooked in abundant water until tender and then drained.

Prepared Creme Fraiche is available at most local markets, usually found among the premium cheeses.

Total time: 30-40 minutes
Serves 4

Heat the water, apple cider vinegar and about 2 tsp salt to boiling and add farro. Reduce heat to medium low and partially cover.

Cook for 25-30 minutes or until farro is tender to the bite. Keep an eye on the farro and add additional water as necessary to ensure farro remains submerged in water during cooking.

Once farro is at desired doneness, add asparagus or snap peas and cook 3 more minutes, adding water if necessary to cover.

Drain farro and vegetables. Immediately return to the pot and stir in olive oil and creme fraiche.

Before serving, squeeze 1/2 a lemon over the farro (or more, to taste), and sprinkle with dill and salt, to taste.

Submitted by: Brian Augusta, The Sacramento Bee

Favorite thing about this recipe: No fuss recipe with both whole grains and fresh, tender-crisp veggies.

Sticky Beans

photo on page 101

- 53-oz can Van Camp's pork and beans, undrained
- 12-oz jar Allied Old English Homade Chili Sauce
- 1 cup brown sugar
- 2 Tbsp Worcestershire sauce
- 2 tsp chili powder
- 1/4 cup dark molasses (unsulfured)
- 2 Tbsp apple cider vinegar
- 1/2 lb Hillshire Farms skinless sausage, sliced into 3/8-inch rounds (optional)

Total time: 1 hour, 45 minutes
Serves 8-10

Heat oven to 350 F.

In a large bowl, combine all ingredients. Mix thoroughly. Pour into a 13x9-inch pan. Bake for about 1 1/2 hours until just slightly thick and sticky. Use as a side dish at a party or barbecue.

If using as a main dish, add the optional sausage to the baking pan by placing the rounds on top of the beans prior to baking. Sink the sausage below the beans and bake as described above.

Submitted by: Rick Tibben, The Tribune (San Luis Obispo)

Favorite thing about this recipe: Everyone loves the taste and texture.

Deviled Peppers

- 6 jalapeño peppers, seeds and ribs removed if desired
- 3 slices bacon
- 1/4 cup mayonnaise
- 1 tsp white vinegar
- 1 tsp yellow mustard
- 1/8 tsp salt
- Pepper
- 6 eggs, hard-boiled

Total time: 30-45 minutes
Serves 12

Heat oven to 375 F.

Cut peppers in half lengthwise. Bake on cookie sheet for 20 minutes.

Fry bacon until crisp, then crumble.

Prepare egg mixture: Mix mayonnaise, vinegar, mustard, salt and pepper. Add eggs. Add crumbled bacon. Mix until well blended and smooth.

Stuff peppers with egg mixture.

Submitted by: Jack Jackson, The Kansas City Star

Favorite thing about this recipe: Blending deviled eggs with jalapeño flavor.

Potato and Sweet Potato Kees

photo on page 97

- 3 cups potatoes, washed and grated coarsely with peels
- 3 cups sweet potatoes or yams, washed and grated coarsely with peels
- 6 Tbsp vegetable oil
- 5 dried red chilies, broken in half (use fewer chilies for a milder dish) or fresh green chilies, diced small
- 3 tsp cumin seeds
- 1 bay leaf
- 1 cup dry-roasted peanuts, ground coarsely
- 2 tsp salt
- 1/4 tsp sugar
- Fresh cilantro, chopped (reserve some for garnish)

Total time: 30 minutes
Serves 6

Gently squeeze grated potatoes to remove excess water and starch.

In a thick, cast-iron skillet, heat oil and add chilies, cumin seeds and the bay leaf, stirring constantly. When cumin seeds turn dark brown, add potatoes and stir.

Turn heat to low, cover and cook, stirring occasionally at first and more often as the kees (shredded potato) starts to cook and tends to stick to the pan. The trick is to use as little oil as possible but attain the crispy texture and flavor that makes this a go-to dish.

After 3-4 minutes — when the potatoes are cooked — stir in peanuts, salt, sugar and fresh cilantro. Cover and cook, stirring occasionally, more often as the potatoes cook and the oil gets absorbed into them.

Cook until done (about 12 minutes) and taste to make sure they are cooked but not too soft. If the potatoes stick to the pan, add more oil.

Garnish with chopped cilantro, a squeeze of lemon juice and a scoop of plain yogurt.

Kees is a wonderful complement and side to meat dishes and can accompany sausage and eggs for breakfast in lieu of hash browns. Also wonderful for a quick midmorning or afternoon snack.

Variations can be made with just potatoes or just sweet potatoes. The version made with all sweet potatoes or yam is really delicious, has a unique flavor, and is particularly good served with baked ham.

Submitted by: Hemalata Dandekar, The Tribune (San Luis Obispo)

Favorite thing about this recipe: Easy to make, and has spicy potatoes and peanuts. What more could one want for a satisfying snack when the munchies hit. I love this dish with meals or by itself with some plain yogurt. Great leftovers in the microwave. Freezes well.

A version of this recipe will be published alongside more than 100 other culinary delights in the extensively revised second edition of Dandekar's "Beyond Curry: Quick and Easy Indian Cooking" (June 2021 Planetizen Press).

Ray's Macaroni Salad

- 1/2 large onion, diced
- 6 eggs, hard-boiled, diced
- 8-10 large sweet gherkin pickles, diced
- 1 box medium shell macaroni
- 1 1/2 cups mayonnaise, plus 1/2 cup more if needed after resting
- 1 Tbsp granulated garlic
- 1/2 tsp Morton Nature's Seasoning
- 1/2 tsp paprika

Total time: 1 hour, 15 minutes
Serves 6-8

In a large mixing bowl, place onions, boiled eggs and pickles.

Cook macaroni to al dente. Drain macaroni and run cold water over it to stop the cooking process. When water feels cold running out of bottom of strainer, shake excess water out of strainer and add macaroni in mixing bowl.

To pasta, add mayonnaise, garlic and Nature's Seasoning to bowl and stir well. Let rest covered in refrigerator for 1 hour. Check to see if more mayonnaise is needed as the macaroni will soak up some of the mayonnaise. If satisfied at the results, sprinkle the paprika over top of the salad. Don't stir it in.

Submitted by: Raymond Denison, The News Tribune (Tacoma)

Favorite thing about this recipe: The taste and texture. The nuttiness of the paprika.

Smoked Salmon Spread

- 1 lb smoked salmon, divided in half
- 16 oz cream cheese, room temperature
- 1 cup mayonnaise
- 1/2 Tbsp Dijon mustard
- 1/2 Tbsp lemon juice
- 1/2 Tbsp horseradish
- 1 tsp dill weed
- Black pepper

Total time: 20 minutes
Serves 15-20

In a food processor, blend the cream cheese and 1/2 the smoked salmon until smooth. Add the mayonnaise, lemon juice, mustard and horseradish and process. Add the dill weed and a pinch of pepper. Process until incorporated. Transfer the mixture to a bowl.

Chop the remaining smoked salmon and stir into the spread until blended. Serve with crackers.

Submitted by: Diane Edison, The News Tribune (Tacoma)

Favorite thing about this recipe: The amazing taste.

Rhubarb Appetizer Spread

- 8 oz cream cheese, softened
- 1/2 cup green onions, thinly sliced
- 1/2 cup sweetened, flaked coconut
- 1/2 cup sliced almonds, divided
- 1/2 cup rhubarb chutney or any fruit chutney

Total time: 20 minutes
Serves 12

In a flat-bottomed serving bowl, spread out the cream cheese evenly. Sprinkle green onions over the cream cheese layer. Layer the coconut evenly over the onions and top with a layer of almonds, saving 2 Tbsp for garnish.

Spread the rhubarb chutney for a top layer. Refrigerate several hours to meld the flavors.

To serve, bring to room temperature and top with the reserved almonds.

Submitted by: Diane Edison,
The News Tribune (Tacoma)

Favorite thing about this recipe: Using chutney and the melding of flavors.

Savory Green Beans

- 1 clove garlic, minced
- 1/4 cup onion, chopped
- 1 Tbsp olive oil
- 1 medium tomato, chopped
- 1 can green beans, drained but reserve 1/2 the liquid
- Salt and pepper

Total time: 15 minutes
Serves 4

Saute garlic and onion in olive oil until translucent. Add chopped tomato to garlic/onion mixture. Stir until the tomato softens and makes a sauce. Stir in the green beans in the sauce.

Add a little of the liquid if needed. Add salt and pepper to your taste.

Submitted by: Sue Horton,
The News Tribune (Tacoma)

Favorite thing about this recipe: The taste is expensive but so easy to prepare.

Creamy Crunchy Cucumber Pea Salad

photo on page 97

- 1 cucumber
- 12 oz frozen peas, thawed and well-drained
- 3 green onions
- 1/2 cup celery, diced
- 4 oz cheddar or Colby cheese, diced pea-size
- 3-4 strips bacon, cooked crisp, crumbled
- 1/4 cup mayonnaise
- 1/4 cup sour cream
- 1/2 tsp dried dill weed
- Salt and pepper

Total time: 30 minutes
Serves 6

Stripe the cucumber by removing long strips of peel with a paring knife, peeler or vegetable stripper (or peel entirely, if you wish).

Slice the cucumber in half lengthwise and run the edge of a spoon down the length to scoop out the seeds. Cut into long strips then cut cross-wise into pea-size dice. Drain well.

Combine cucumber with remaining ingredients, reserving some of the green onion tops and bacon for garnish.

Stir until well-coated with dressing. Add salt and pepper to taste.

Garnish with reserved onions and bacon. Chill before serving.

Submitted by: Peg Bowman, The Wichita Eagle

Favorite thing about this recipe: I like that this make-ahead salad has the right balance of creamy and crunchy, made even better with cheese and bacon.

Gourmet Potatoes

- 6 medium potatoes
- 2 cups cheddar cheese, shredded
- 4 Tbsp butter, divided
- 1 1/2 cup sour cream, room temperature
- 1/3 cup onion, chopped
- 1 tsp salt
- 1/4 tsp pepper

Total time: 40-60 minutes
Serves 8

Cook potatoes in skins. Cool and peel, then shred coarsely. You can cook the potatoes the day before if needed.

Heat oven to 350 F. In a saucepan over low heat, combine cheese and 2 Tbsp butter, stirring occasionally until almost melted. Remove from heat and blend in sour cream, onion, salt and pepper.

Fold in potatoes, turn out into a greased 2-quart casserole. Dot with remaining butter, bake 25 minutes or until heated through.

Recipe can be doubled or tripled.

Submitted by: Sandra Berkowitz, The Herald-Sun

Favorite thing about this recipe: A family favorite at the holidays!

Desserts

Bourbon Cinnamon Pecan Bundt Cake

photo on page 107

Pecan Outer Crust

- 1/2 cup unsalted butter, melted
- 1/2 cup brown sugar
- 3 Tbsp corn syrup
- 1 cup pecan halves, plus extra for garnish

Cake

- 3 cups all-purpose flour
- 1/4 tsp baking soda
- 2 3/4 tsp baking powder
- 1 tsp salt
- 1 tsp cinnamon
- 1 1/2 cups unsalted butter, softened
- 2 cups granulated sugar
- 1 large egg
- 3 large egg whites
- 1 tsp vanilla extract
- 1/4 cup bourbon

Chocolate Ganache Topping

- 1 cup semisweet chocolate chips
- 1/3 cup heavy whipping cream

Total time: 1 hour, 30 minutes
Serves 12-16

Heat oven to 350 F. Grease 10-inch non-stick Bundt cake pan of choice.

Make the pecan outer crust: In a bowl, combine melted butter, brown sugar and corn syrup. Mix well.

Stir the pecans into the mixture until all are coated with the brown sugar mixture. Pour the mixture into the Bundt cake pan and set aside.

Make the cake: In a medium bowl, add flour, baking soda, baking powder, salt and cinnamon. Mix together and set aside.

In a large bowl, cream unsalted butter and granulated sugar with electric mixer on medium for 2-3 minutes until you have a whipped, creamy texture.

To large bowl, add large egg and mix until combined. Mix in additional egg whites until combined with butter sugar mixture.

Next, to large bowl, add in vanilla and bourbon. Combine all ingredients well still using an electric mixer.

In large bowl, add about 1/2 of the mixed dry ingredients. Combine well with a mixing spoon. Repeat for the second half of the dry ingredients.

When all the ingredients have been combined well, add batter into greased cake pan on top of crust mixture and bake for 40-50 minutes. Let cake cool completely before adding chocolate ganache.

Make the chocolate ganache: In bowl, add chocolate chips and heavy whipping cream. Heat in microwave for 45-60 seconds.

Stir cream and chocolate chips slowly until it turns into a thick ganache.

Pour on cooled cake and garnish with extra pecans, if desired.

Submitted by: Kimberly Pina, National Winner — The Kansas City Star

Favorite thing about this recipe: The flavor is amazing once the alcohol bakes out.

Pumpkin Flan

photo on page 104

Caramel

- 3/4 cup granulated sugar
- 1/3 cup maple syrup
- 1/2 tsp sea salt

Flan

- 14-oz can sweetened condensed milk
- 12-oz can evaporated milk
- 15-oz can Libby's Pure Pumpkin
- 1/2 cup whole milk ricotta cheese
- 4 jumbo eggs
- 1 tsp vanilla extract
- 1 Tbsp maple syrup
- 1 Tbsp orange juice
- 1/2 tsp cinnamon
- 1/2 tsp nutmeg
- 1/2 tsp allspice
- Pinch of sea salt

Total time: 1 hour, 30 minutes to 2 hours
Serves 8-10

Heat oven to 350 F. and set a rack in the middle position.

Use an 8-inch round cake pan, do not use a springform. Can also be made in ramekins for individual servings.

Make the caramel: In a heavy saucepan over medium-high heat, add the sugar, syrup, salt and 1/3 cup of very hot water. Stir well.

When the mixture begins to boil, reduce the heat to a bare simmer. Allow the mix to cook, without stirring, until golden brown, (about 230 F on a candy thermometer).

Carefully pour caramel into the cake pan and set aside.

Make the flan: In a large mixing bowl, combine the two milks, pumpkin and ricotta. Using a hand or stick mixer with a whisk attachment, beat the ingredients at low speed until smooth and uniform.

Add all other ingredients, and whisk on low to fully incorporate.

Use a spatula to transfer the batter from bowl to pan.

Place the cake pan a roasting pan, and carefully fill that with hot water to roughly halfway up your pan.

Bake for 60-70 minutes, until the flan has set, but still has some jiggle to the middle. A toothpick inserted into the flan should come out clean.

Remove flan from oven, and from the roasting pan, and transfer to a cooling rack.

Allow the flan to cool completely, then cover the pan tightly with plastic wrap and refrigerate for at least 4 hours.

When ready to serve, run a knife around the edge of the pan, and place a serving plate tight to your pan. Quickly but gently give the pan a flip and voilà! Add whipped cream, if desired.

Submitted by: Eben Atwater, Local Winner — The Bellingham Herald

Favorite thing about this recipe: It's a beautiful pumpkin flavor, but a little unusual, and it's just gorgeous.

Cranberry Citrus Olive Oil Cake

- Freshly grated zest from 1 lemon and 1 orange
- 1 1/3 cup sugar
- 2 3/4 cups whole wheat flour, plus extra for dusting the cake pan
- 1 tsp baking powder
- 1 tsp fine sea salt
- 1/2 tsp baking soda
- 12-oz bag cranberries
- 3 eggs, room temperature
- 1 cup whole milk
- 1 cup extra-virgin olive oil

Total time: 1 hour, 20 minutes
Serves 12

Heat oven to 350 F. Adjust oven rack to the center of the oven.

Spray a nonstick 12-cup fluted (Bundt) cake pan with cooking spray or lightly coat with olive oil. Dust with flour.

In a large bowl, combine citrus zests and sugar. Use your fingers to gently crush and coat the zest with sugar (your hands will smell amazing).

To same bowl, add the flour, baking powder, salt and baking soda and whisk until blended. Stir in the cranberries.

In a medium bowl, lightly beat the eggs. Add the milk, then whisk in the olive oil in a slow stream until blended. Pour olive oil mixture over the dry ingredients, stirring until the batter is smooth. Pour the batter into the prepared pan.

Bake 45-55 minutes. A toothpick inserted into the cake should come out dry.

Cool the pan on a rack for 2 hours before unmolding.

Submitted by: Mary Glen, Local Winner — Idaho Statesman

Favorite thing about this recipe: The combination of cranberry, sugar and citrus.

Pumpkin Spice Doughnut Bread Pudding with Rum-Raisin Sauce

Bread Pudding

- 8 eggs
- 3 cups milk
- 1 cup fresh pumpkin puree (or canned mashed pumpkin)
- 1 cup light brown sugar, packed
- 5 1/3 Tbsp butter, melted
- 1 1/2 tsp ground cinnamon
- 1 1/2 tsp vanilla extract
- 1/4 tsp ground nutmeg
- 6 large glazed doughnuts, cut into 3/4-inch pieces (about 6 cups pieces)

Rum-Raisin Sauce

- 1/2 cup butter
- 1/2 cup brown sugar, packed
- 1 Tbsp cornstarch
- 1/2 cup half-and-half
- 1/3 cup golden raisins
- 1/4 cup rum

Total time: 1 hour
Serves 10-12

Note

Apple juice or white grape juice can be substituted for rum, if desired.

Bread Pudding

Heat oven to 350 F.

In a large bowl, lightly beat eggs with a whisk; add milk and next 6 ingredients, and whisk until blended. Add doughnut pieces, and toss gently until coated; let stand 3 minutes.

Spoon mixture into lightly greased 13x9-inch baking dish.

Bake for 45-50 minutes or until puffed and lightly browned. Serve immediately.

Sauce

In saucepan, melt butter; add brown sugar, stirring until sugar dissolves.

Add cornstarch to half-and-half, whisking until blended.

Whisk half-and-half mixture into butter mixture; add raisins.

Cook, whisking constantly, until slightly thickened and bubbly. Remove from heat, and whisk in rum.

Serve warm. Yields 1 1/2 cups sauce.

Submitted by: Susan Dobbs, Local Winner — Ledger-Enquirer (Columbus)

Favorite thing about this recipe:
Doughnuts are typically served for breakfast and bread pudding for dessert, so this marriage of the two is perfect for either occasion. It also makes a grand brunch finale.

Apple Pie Squares

photo on page 108

- 1 cup, plus 1 1/2 Tbsp all-purpose flour, sifted, divided
- 1 scant cup rolled oats
- 3/4 cup brown sugar, packed
- 1/2 cup butter
- 1/2 tsp cinnamon
- 5 medium apples, peeled and sliced, Fuji or other cooking apple (about 5 cups)
- 1 tsp cinnamon
- 1/4 cup granulated sugar

Total time: 1 hour, 30 minutes
Serves 9

Heat oven to 350 F. Spray 8x8 pan with cooking oil.

In bowl, combine first 5 ingredients to make crumb mixture. Divide in half.

Press 1/2 of crumb mixture in bottom of prepared 8x8.

Combine remaining ingredients, stirring until apples are coated. Layer apple mixture on top of crumb mixture. Sprinkle remaining crumb mixture over apples distributing equally.

Bake for 55-60 minutes or until apples are bubbly and crumb mixture is starting to brown.

Cut into squares and serve warm with vanilla ice cream.

Submitted by: Martha Thompson, Local Winner — Lexington Herald-Leader

Favorite thing about this recipe: The blended taste of apples, cinnamon and oats.

Aunt June's Banana Pudding

photo on page 112

- 14-oz can sweetened condensed milk
- 1 1/2 cups cold water
- 3.4-oz package instant vanilla pudding
- 1 pint whipping cream
- Vanilla wafers (as many as you want)
- 3 bananas, sliced and dipped in lemon juice

Total time: 20 minutes
Serves 4-6

In bowl, combine sweetened condensed milk and water, add pudding mix and beat well. Chill 5 minutes.

While mixture is chilling, whip the whipping cream.

Fold whipped cream into the pudding mix. Layer pudding, wafers and bananas into desired serving dishes.

Chill thoroughly, enjoy and think of me!

Submitted by: Shana Singer, The News Tribune (Tacoma)

Favorite thing about this recipe: The simplicity and reminder of being a kid.

Heavenly Pistachio Cake with Cherry Icing

Cake

- Bundt pan
- Flour, for dusting pan
- Shortening, for greasing pan
- One 15.25-oz box yellow cake mix
- 3.4-oz package instant pistachio pudding
- 1 1/2 cups water
- 1/4 cup vegetable oil
- 4 eggs
- 1/2 tsp almond extract
- Green food coloring

Icing

- 2 cups powdered sugar
- 2 Tbsp butter, melted
- 3 Tbsp maraschino cherry juice

Total time: 1 hour, 20 minutes
Serves 10

Heat oven to 350 F.

Prepare 10-cup Bundt pan with shortening and dust with flour. Tap and discard excess flour.

In large bowl, combine cake mix, pistachio pudding, water and oil. Using electric mixer on low speed until combined. Add eggs, one at a time. Add almond extract and 7 drops of the green food coloring. Blend and mix on medium speed for 2 minutes.

Pour cake batter in prepared Bundt pan.

Bake 50-55 minutes, or until toothpick comes out clean.

Cool cake in Bundt pan for 20 minutes.

Remove cake and place on decorative cake plate. Cool cake completely for 45 minutes.

Make icing: Mix powdered sugar with melted butter. Add cherry juice. Consistency should be on the thick side. Spread on top of cake.

Submitted by: Carol Melgosa, Merced Sun-Star

Favorite thing about this recipe: Display beautiful cake on decorative and vintage pedestal cake plates. My dear friends are gifted with a vintage cake plate with this beautiful and delicious cake. I have over 95 vintage cake plates, that I collect to "gift" someone special.

White Chocolate Bread Pudding with White Chocolate and Raspberry Sauces

Bread Pudding

- 1 Tbsp butter or margarine
- 1/2 cup sugar, plus 2-3 tsp for coating pan
- 6 cups bread cubes (French bread is recommended)
- 2 tsp vanilla
- 2 large eggs
- 1 tsp cinnamon
- 2 cups heavy whipping cream
- 6 oz white chocolate, coarsely chopped

Raspberry Sauce

- 16-oz jar seedless red raspberry jam

White Chocolate Sauce

- 12 oz white chocolate, coarsely chopped
- 3/4 cup heavy whipping cream
- 1 Tbsp, plus 1 tsp light corn syrup

Total time: 1 hour, 15 minutes
Serves 9

Bread Pudding

Heat oven to 350 F. Coat 8x8 glass baking dish with butter or margarine, and sprinkle with 2-3 tsp sugar.

In large mixing bowl, place bread cubes.

In a separate bowl, whisk vanilla, eggs and cinnamon and set aside.

In a medium saucepan over medium heat, warm heavy whipping cream with white chocolate and sugar. Bring the mixture to a simmer, while stirring. Immediately remove from heat.

Add the egg mixture to the heavy cream mixture and pour over the torn bread cubes in large bowl.

Cover bread cubes with the combined mixture and transfer to 8x8 baking dish. Cover the dish with foil.

Place the covered baking dish into a larger dish and fill the larger one with enough water to come halfway up the sides of the pudding. Bake for 25 minutes.

Remove the foil and increase the oven temperature to 375 F.

Continue baking for approximately 30 minutes or until the top is golden brown and firm when touched in the middle.

Remove the pudding from the water bath and set aside to cool slightly.

To serve, cut the cooled bread pudding into nine squares. Lightly drizzle tops with white chocolate sauce and raspberry sauce. May garnish with fresh raspberries and basil or mint as desired. Best served warm.

Raspberry Sauce

In a microwave-proof dish, place seedless red raspberry jam and gently heat the jam, stirring to the consistency of a medium sauce. The sauce maybe used to decorate the plate prior to plating the bread pudding as well as used to top the bread pudding.

White Chocolate Sauce

In the top of a double boiler set over barely simmering water, combine the white chocolate and heavy whipping cream. Whisk the chocolate cream mixture until the chocolate is melted and the mixture is smooth. Remove the sauce from the heat and stir in the corn syrup. Set aside to cool to room temperature. Yields 2-3 cups.

Submitted by: Cindy Gordon, Local Winner — The Sun News (Myrtle Beach)

Favorite thing about this recipe: Five-star quality dessert to make at home.

Snickerdoodle Apple Pie Galette

Filling

- 5 cups apples, cored and sliced
- 1/2 lemon, juiced
- 3 cups water
- 1/3 cup cornstarch
- 1/4 tsp salt
- 1 1/3 cups sugar
- 2 tsp cinnamon
- 1 tsp nutmeg
- 1 tsp vanilla

Crust

- 2 1/2 cups flour
- 1 tsp kosher salt
- 1 Tbsp sugar
- 1 cup butter
- 8 Tbsp ice water
- 8 snickerdoodle cookies, crushed and divided
- 1 egg

Total time: 1 hour, 30 minutes
Serves 6-8

Heat oven to 350 F.

In saucepan, add the apple slices and lemon juice.

In measuring cup, mix 3 cups water and cornstarch. Pour over the apples. To the saucepan, also add 1/4 tsp salt, 1 1/3 cups sugar, cinnamon, nutmeg and vanilla.

Bring to a boil over medium heat, stirring occasionally. After 8 minutes, remove from heat to cool.

In a bowl, blend together the flour, 1 tsp salt, 1 Tbsp sugar, butter and ice water until consistent, then flatten into pie tin to make a large pie crust.

Spread 4 of the crushed snickerdoodle cookies over the crust.

Pour apple filling into the crust. Fold over edges to make galette purse. Brush with egg yolk. Sprinkle remaining crushed cookies over the edge of the pie crust.

Bake for 1 hour, until pie is brown.

Submitted by: Jane Bernal, The Modesto Bee

Favorite thing about this recipe: Beautiful finished product, delightful aroma.

Zane's Classic Chocolate Chip Cookies

- 2 1/4 cups pastry or cake flour, sifted
- 1/2 tsp cornstarch
- 1 tsp baking soda
- 1/2 tsp salt
- 1/2 cup granulated sugar
- 1 cup dark brown sugar
- 1/2 cup butter, melted
- 1/2 cup vegetable shortening
- 2 tsp vanilla extract
- 2 large eggs, room temperature
- 1 cup dark chocolate chips
- 1 cup semisweet chocolate chips
- Sea salt

Total time: 35 minutes
Yields 12-14 cookies

Note on Cookie Dough

This recipe is best if cookie dough is chilled for 24-36 hours before baking, however, you may bake cookies as soon as the dough is mixed completely.

If chilling the cookie dough, wrap the dough in plastic wrap and place in a refrigerator safe storage bag. Place in fridge for the recommended time.

To bake after chilling dough: You do not have to chill the baking sheet if following this method.

Heat oven to 350 F. Line 2 baking sheets with parchment paper. Chill baking sheets if baking the same day as making dough.

Retrieve 2 large mixing bowls.

In one mixing bowl, sift the flour, cornstarch, baking soda and salt until fully combined. Set aside.

In the other mixing bowl, sift the granulated and brown sugars until combined. Add melted butter and vegetable shortening to sugar mixture and fold gently with silicone spatula until combined. Add vanilla extract and both eggs — one egg at a time — into sugar mixture until fully combined.

Make a well in the middle of the dry ingredients and slowly pour 1/2 of the wet ingredients into the well. Fold ingredients with spatula until just combined.

Lightly dust the chocolate chips with flour as needed and place the chips into the partially mixed cookie dough. Pour the rest of the wet ingredients into the dough mixture and continue to gently fold with spatula until combined.

Using a spoon, take 2 Tbsp of cookie dough and roll into a ball with your hand. Gently press the cookie dough flat with either your hand, a spoon or the bottom of a drinking glass until shaped (you may also use cookie cutters, if you desire). Place the dough onto the lined baking sheet, keeping dough at least 2-3 inches apart.

Bake for 8 minutes for chewy cookies, or 12 minutes for crispier cookies. Garnish cookies with a pinch of sea salt.

Once cookies are done baking, remove from the oven and let cookies sit on the hot baking sheet for at least 5 minutes. Remove the cookies from the baking sheet and let them cool on wire rack for at least 30 minutes before serving.

Serve with a glass of milk and enjoy!

Submitted by: Sierra Eggum, The Bellingham Herald

Favorite thing about this recipe: It was inspired by my husband!

Blueberry Cobbler

- 4 cups blueberries, frozen or fresh
- 1 cup water
- 1 cup sugar
- 1 tsp vanilla extract
- 1 tsp almond extract
- 1/4 tsp cinnamon
- 1/4 tsp nutmeg
- 4 Tbsp butter
- 4 Tbsp tapioca

Topping
- 1 egg, well beaten
- 1 1/2 cups self-rising flour
- 1/4 cup sugar
- 1/4 cup cooking oil
- 1 1/2 cups milk

Total time: 2 hours
Serves 8

Heat oven to 350 F.

In saucepan, heat blueberries with water and boil for 5 minutes. Remove from heat and pour in 9x12 baking pan.

To the berries, add sugar, vanilla, almond, cinnamon, nutmeg, butter and tapioca. Mix well.

In a bowl, mix egg, flour, sugar, cooking oil and milk to the consistency of pourable pancake mix and pour on top of blueberries.

Bake for 50-60 minutes.

Submitted by: Maxine Ramsay, Sun Herald

Favorite thing about this recipe: We have plenty of blueberries on our small farm.

Apple, Banana, Cranberry, Pecan Morning Bread

photo on page 104

- 2 cups flour
- 3/4 cup sugar
- 1 tsp cinnamon
- 1 tsp baking soda
- 1 tsp baking powder
- 1 tsp salt
- 1/2 cup pecans, chopped
- 1/2 cup dried shaved cranberries (may substitute dried wild blueberries)
- 2 large eggs, lightly beaten, room temperature
- 3/4 cup canola oil
- 2 tsp vanilla
- 2 medium bananas, coarsely mashed
- 1 medium golden delicious apple, peeled, cored and diced

Total time: 1 hour, 45 minutes
Serves 10-12

Heat oven to 325 F.

In medium-size bowl, whisk flour, sugar, cinnamon, baking soda, baking powder and salt, then fold in cranberries and nuts and set aside.

In a large bowl, using a fork, mix eggs, oil, vanilla, bananas and apple.

Mix dry ingredients into wet ingredients 1/3 at a time and combine well.

Pour into a greased 5x9 pan and bake for 75 minutes. Wooden skewer inserted should come out clean.

Cool for 10 minutes in pan, then run knife around bread to remove from pan and cool on wire rack.

Submitted by: Richard Muehlhausen, The Bellingham Herald

Favorite thing about this recipe: Easy to make.

Chocolate Bourbon Pecan Pie

photo on page 108

- Pastry mix
- 1/2 cup butter
- 3 eggs
- 3/4 cup brown sugar
- 3/4 cup dark corn syrup
- 3 tsp vanilla
- 1/2 tsp salt
- 3 Tbsp bourbon (more if desired)
- 2 1/2 cups whole pecans, divided
- 1/3 cup dark chocolate chips

Total time: 2 hours
Serves 8-12

Make pastry according to package and put into the fridge for at least 30 minutes. When cold, roll out, put into pie pan and flute the edges.

Heat oven to 350 F.

Melt butter. In a large bowl, beat the eggs then add the brown sugar and dark corn syrup. Slowly add the melted butter. Add the vanilla, salt and bourbon. Chop 2 cups of the pecans and add.

Pour into an unbaked pie shell. Distribute the dark chocolate chips on top of the filling then arrange the last 1/2 cup of whole pecans. Bake for 45-60 minutes.

Submitted by: Alice Clark, The Bellingham Herald

Favorite thing about this recipe: Because I believe if you're going to eat a slice of pecan pie, you might as well go for it. Adding bourbon and dark chocolate takes the pie to a totally different level of decadence.

Cherry Ribbon Pie

- 9-inch pastry shell, baked and cooled
- 14-oz can sweetened condensed milk
- 1/2 cup fresh lemon juice
- 2 cups Cool Whip
- 1 can cherry pie filling

Total time: 1 hour, 10 minutes
Serves 8

Combine condensed milk and lemon juice. Fold in Cool Whip. Spread 1/3 into pastry shell. Spread cherry pie filling, top with remaining topping. Chill 1 hour and enjoy.

Submitted by: Ariele Gilbert, The Bellingham Herald

Favorite thing about this recipe: It's delicious.

Mary Lou's Strawberry Rhubarb Custard Pie

- 1 Pillsbury Pie Crust
- 1 Tbsp flour
- 3 eggs
- 1 cup milk
- 1 3/4 cup sugar, plus 2 Tbsp for coating crust
- 4 cups rhubarb, sliced
- 16 oz fresh strawberries, rinsed and halved

Total time: 1 hour, 45 minutes
Serves 12-15

Heat oven to 325 F.

Spray 9x13 pan with cooking spray. Place pie crust on bottom and sides of pan.

Sprinkle 1 Tbsp flour and 2 Tbsp sugar on the bottom of pie crust and mix.

In bowl, beat eggs, milk and sugar. Add rhubarb to egg mixture and mix. Add strawberries.

Pour into a 9x13 pan and mix.

Bake 1 hour and 15 minutes.

Submitted by: Mary Lou Wittenauer, Belleville News-Democrat

Favorite thing about this recipe: The strawberries and rhubarb have a unique sweet and sour type of taste.

Simple Old-Fashioned Rhubarb Cake

- 1 cup oil or shortening
- 1 1/2 cups sugar
- 3 eggs
- 1 Tbsp vanilla
- 1/2 tsp salt
- 1 tsp cinnamon
- 1 tsp baking soda
- 2 cups flour
- 1 cup walnuts or pecans, coarsely chopped
- 4 cups rhubarb, diced (frozen is okay)

Total time: 1 hour, 30 minutes
Serves 15-20

Heat oven to 350 F.

Mix all ingredients in order given, mixing well after each addition.

Pour into well-greased 8x10 baking pan and bake for 55 minutes.

Best if served warm with whipped cream or ice cream. Store in refrigerator for best results.

Submitted by: Patty Hamm, Idaho Statesman

Favorite thing about this recipe: I take this to a lot of potlucks and am always being asked for the recipe. The rhubarb gives it a bit of a tart flavor, but it is just sweet enough to balance it out for a wonderful dessert that is not too heavy.

Coconut Sour Cream Cake

- Yellow cake mix (for six-layer cake use three boxes of cake)
- Eggs
- Butter, melted
- Heavy cream
- 24 oz sugar
- 24-oz container sour cream
- 16-oz package shredded coconut
- Cool Whip (with vanilla)

Total time: 1 hour, plus 3 days
Serves 10

Cake

Make cake as package directions with these adjustments:

- Add an extra egg
- Use melted butter instead of oil
- Use heavy cream instead of water plus a little more cream than water advised on cake recipe.

When cake is cooked, put in freezer until frozen or almost frozen. Slice each cake layer in half. Layer with filling (it will be large and ugly). Frost with Cool Whip and sprinkle coconut on top.

Most importantly, put cake in airtight container and refrigerate or freeze for at least three days. This lets the flavors blend.

Filling

Mix equal parts of sugar and sour cream — so one container of sour cream to same amount of sugar. Mix until sugar is not grainy. Add coconut to make a thick filling.

Submitted by: Julie Stevens, Idaho Statesman

Favorite thing about this recipe: Letting the cake sit for three days lets the flavors marry and is delicious.

Way-Spicy Holiday Spice Balls

- 2 cups whole wheat flour
- 1 tsp baking powder
- 1/2 tsp baking soda
- 1/2 tsp salt
- 1 Tbsp ground ginger
- 1 Tbsp ground cinnamon
- 1 tsp ground cloves
- 1 tsp ground allspice
- 1 tsp ground nutmeg
- 1 tsp ground cardamom
- 1/2 cup crystallized ginger, chopped
- 1/4 cup vegetable oil
- 1/3 cup dark molasses
- 1/4 cup sugar
- 1 egg
- 1 tsp vanilla
- Powdered sugar for dipping

Total time: 1 hour, 15 minutes
Yields 3 dozen

In bowl, stir flour, baking powder, baking soda, salt, spices and chopped ginger together.

In a separate larger bowl, beat together oil, molasses, sugar, egg and vanilla. Add flour mixture a bit at time, stirring, until just blended.

Form stiff batter into ball, wrap in wax paper or greased plastic wrap and chill for 30 minutes or longer.

Heat oven to 375 F.

Line baking sheet with parchment paper. Pinch off chunks from big ball, rolling into balls a bit less than 1 inch in circumference, dip one half in powdered sugar, and place about 2 inches apart on baking sheet.

Refrigerate dough ball between baking batches.

Bake 10-12 minutes. Cool on rack.

Submitted by: Anne Hoag, Centre Daily Times

Favorite thing about this recipe: With a heavier dose of spices, more of an adult cookie. Just one usually satisfies a holiday sweet tooth.

Black Forest Cheesecake

photo on page 108

- Three 8-oz packages cream cheese, softened
- 14-oz can sweetened condensed milk
- 3 eggs
- 2 tsp vanilla extract
- 2 Oreo pie crusts, store-bought or homemade
- 1 can cherry pie filling

Total time: 1 hour, 50 minutes
Yields 2 cheesecakes

Heat oven to 300 F.

In a large mixing bowl, beat cream cheese until fluffy. Gradually beat in condensed milk until smooth. Add eggs one at a time and mix in between. Add vanilla extract. Mix well.

Pour into the two pie crusts. Bake for 45-60 minutes. Allow to cool for 30 minutes (in the freezer) or overnight (in the refrigerator).

When cooled, add cherry pie filling on top and spread evenly over the surface.

Submitted by: Gabby Young, The Island Packet

Favorite thing about this recipe: It can be altered to tasted and if you are making a homemade crust you can add the Oreo cream to the filling and it is delicious.

Italian Biscotti (Anisette Toast)

- 6 eggs
- 1 Tbsp anise extract
- 1/2 tsp salt
- 1 cup canola oil
- 1 cup sugar
- 5 cups all-purpose flour
- 4 tsp baking powder

Total time: 25 minutes
Yields 12 cookies

Heat oven to 350 F.

Mix first 5 ingredients then add flour and baking powder.

Divide into 3 flat loaves (2x6).

Bake until golden in color. Remove from oven and slice on a 45-degree angle and turn each on side. Bake again until golden brown on all sides.

Leave plain or sift with powdered sugar. Stays great 5 to 7 days.

Submitted by: Dianne Powell, Bradenton Herald

Favorite thing about this recipe: Very addictive if you like licorice!

Mini Caramel Filled Pumpkin Cakes with Salted Almonds

photo on page 106

Cake Batter

- 2/3 cup butter
- 2 2/3 cups sugar
- 4 eggs
- 16-oz can pumpkin puree
- 2/3 cup water
- 3 1/3 cups self-rising flour
- 1 tsp cinnamon
- 1 tsp ground cloves

Caramel Topping

- 1 cup sugar
- 1/4 cup water
- 2 Tbsp corn syrup
- 3/4 cup cream
- 4 Tbsp butter

Toasted Almonds

- 2 Tbsp butter
- 3/4 cup Marcona almonds, roughly chopped
- 1 tsp sea salt

Total time: 55 minutes
Serves 12

Heat oven to 350 F.

Grease and flour 12 mini-Bundt pans (or 1 large Bundt pan).

In a large bowl, mix butter and sugar until well combined. Add eggs, pumpkin and water. Blend in flour and spices.

Bake minicakes for about 30 minutes or until wooden pick inserted in center comes out clean. Bake full-size cake 1 hour.

Remove from oven to rack for cooling. Remove from pan after 10 minutes.

Make caramel topping: In a small pan, combine sugar, water and corn syrup. Boil on high heat until the mixture turns to an amber color — about 6 minutes. Whisk in cream and butter. Continue cooking until mixture thickens. It will continue to thicken as it cools.

Toast almonds: In a large skillet, melt butter over medium heat. Add chopped nuts and cook, stirring frequently, until nuts turn golden brown. Remove from skillet to paper towel and immediately sprinkle with sea salt.

To serve: Place individual Bundt cake on serving plate. Fill center hole with caramel topping allowing it to run down sides of cake and puddle on plate. Top with about 1 Tbsp of salted almonds.

For large Bundt cake, drizzle caramel over cake and sprinkle evenly with toasted almonds. Slice to serve.

Submitted by: Mary Leverette, The State

Favorite thing about this recipe: The flavors are exceptional!

Delicious Country Custard

- 1 cup sugar
- 2 Tbsp all-purpose flour
- 2 eggs, slightly beaten
- 6 Tbsp margarine, melted
- 1 cup buttermilk
- 2 tsp vanilla extract
- 1 Pillsbury Pet-Ritz Deep Dish Pie Crust, uncooked

Total time: 1 hour, 40 minutes
Serves 6

Preheat oven to 400 F.

In a large bowl add sugar, flour, eggs, margarine, buttermilk and vanilla extract. Stir after adding each ingredient.

Bake in a 9-inch uncooked Pillsbury Pet-Ritz Deep Dish Pie Crust for 10 minutes. Then reduce oven temperature to 325 F and bake for 30 minutes.

Pie will be golden brown when cooked. Makes 1 deep dish pie.

Submitted by: Patricia Carrington, The Herald-Sun

Favorite thing about this recipe: The taste is amazing and the look is appealing.

Strawberry Pizza

photo on page 104

- Sugar cookie dough, homemade recipe or 16-oz store-bought
- Two 8-oz packages cream cheese, softened
- 3/4 cup powdered sugar
- 1 tsp vanilla extract
- 2 pints fresh strawberries
- 14 oz strawberry glaze, homemade recipe or store-bought

Total time: 30-45 minutes
Serves 12-16

Make sugar cookie crust: Spread sugar cookie dough onto cookie sheet, less than 1/2-inch thick. Bake as directed and cool.

Make cream cheese filling: Mix softened cream cheese with powdered sugar (to taste) and vanilla until creamy.

Spread filling onto cooled cookie crust.

Make fruit topping: Clean and rinse strawberries. Cut or the slice strawberries, mix with strawberry glaze and spread on top of prepared cream cheese

Chill 1 hour and enjoy.

Submitted by: Phyllis Zavala, The Fresno Bee

Favorite thing about this recipe: Easy and delicious.

Pistachio Nut Cookies

photo on page 109

- 1/2 cup butter
- 1/2 cup sugar
- 1/2 cup brown sugar
- 1 egg
- 1 1/2 tsp vanilla
- 1 1/2 cup flour
- 1 cup honey-roasted pistachios, shelled

Total time: 20 minutes
Yields 2 dozen medium cookies

Heat oven to 350 F.

Cream butter, sugar and brown sugar together. Add egg and vanilla, mix well. Add flour and mix together. Mix in honey roasted pistachio meats.

Place 1 Tbsp spoonfuls of mix on a greased cookie sheet and bake for about 10-12 minutes.

Submitted by: Barbara Schaad, The Fresno Bee

Favorite thing about this recipe: My favorite thing about these cookies is the healthy pistachio meats, not only because they are healthy for you but because my husband and I are the actual growers of these pistachios. It's nice to have a cookie recipe that has some healthy nutritional value to them and you don't feel so guilty for having one (or two)!

Pumpkin Cake

photo on page 112

- 1 box yellow cake mix
- 1 cup butter, divided
- 4 eggs, divided
- 1 large can pumpkin
- 1 small can evaporated milk
- 2 cups sugar, divided
- 2 tsp pumpkin spice
- 1/2 tsp salt
- 1 cup flour
- 1 tsp baking powder

Total time: 1 hour, 20 minutes
Serves 24

Heat oven to 325 F.

Make crust: In bowl, combine cake mix with 1/2 cup melted butter and 1 egg. Mix until blended. Pat in bottom of large oblong baking dish.

Make filling: Mix pumpkin, evaporated milk, 2 beaten eggs, 1 cup sugar, pumpkin spice and salt until well combined. Pour over cake (crust).

Make topping: Mix 1 cup flour, 1 tsp baking powder, 1/2 cup sugar, 1 egg. Mix until crumbly. Put on top of filling.

Melt 1/2 cup butter and spoon on topping.

Bake for 55 minutes.

Submitted by: Nelsene DeRanian, The Fresno Bee

Favorite thing about this recipe: The ease and fun of the prep ... and best of all, the taste!

Oatmeal Date-Nut Cookies

- 1 cup granulated sugar
- 1 cup brown sugar
- 1 cup oil
- 1 tsp vanilla
- 2 large eggs
- 3/4 cup chopped dates, moistened with 3 Tbsp boiling water
- 2 cups flour
- 1 tsp baking soda
- 1 tsp baking powder
- 1/2 tsp salt
- 3/4 cup nuts, chopped
- 3 cups quick oatmeal

Total time: 1 hour, 30 minutes
Yields 3 1/2-4 dozen cookies

Heat oven to 350 F.

Mix granulated and brown sugars, oil, vanilla and eggs. Add moistened dates.

Add flour, baking soda, baking powder, salt. Mix well.

Add chopped nuts. Add oatmeal, 1 cup at a time.

Drop by tsp on lightly oiled cookie sheet. Bake 10-12 minutes until light brown.

Cool for a few minutes in pan before removing to cooling rack.

Submitted by: Connie Coberly, The Fresno Bee

Favorite thing about this recipe: Its deep flavor and moistness.

Pistachio Mousse

- 2 cups whipping cream
- 1/2 cup powdered sugar
- 2 tsp vanilla
- 2 tsp almond extract
- 1 cup pistachio nuts, chopped
- Green food coloring

Total time: 5 hours
Serves 6-8

Whip cream stiff, fold in sugar, flavorings and nuts.

Lightly mix in a drop or two of food coloring.

Pile lightly in an ice cube tray, or freeze in equal parts of salt and ice, similar to the mixture you would use in an ice cream maker.

Submitted by: Chris Clemons, The Fresno Bee

Favorite thing about this recipe: It was Grandma's recipe.

Triple Treat Cocoa Cakes

photo on page 104

Cake

- 3 very ripe bananas
- 1 cup sugar
- 1/2 cup almond milk, room temperature
- 1/4 cup peanut butter
- 1/2 cup cocoa powder, unsweetened
- 1/2 tsp salt
- 3/4 tsp baking soda
- 1 1/4 tsp baking powder
- 1 1/2 cups flour
- 1/4 cup chocolate chips
- 1/3 cup pecans, chopped

Maple Butter Frosting

- 1/2 cup butter
- 2 cups powdered sugar
- 1 Tbsp maple syrup

Total time: 30 minutes
Serves 12

Heat oven to 350 F.

Mash bananas. Add sugar, almond milk and peanut butter. Using mixer, beat until smooth.

In separate bowl, combine cocoa powder, salt, baking soda, baking powder and flour. Sift or spoon into banana mixture, folding in after each addition until incorporated. Add chocolate chips and stir again.

Place 12 cupcake holders on a baking sheet or in a muffin pan. Spoon in batter.

Bake 20-22 minutes. Remove and cool.

Toast pecans in 350 F oven for 5-7 minutes; cool as cocoa cakes cool.

Maple Butter Frosting: Once pecans and cocoa cakes are cool, whip butter. Add powdered sugar and maple syrup. Continue to whip. Pipe or spread over cocoa cakes.

Sprinkle toasted pecans over top of each cake.

Submitted by: Hazel Cooper, The Fresno Bee

Favorite thing about this recipe: This triple treat uses peanut butter instead of oil and is as quick to make as it is delicious. Real maple syrup gives the frosting a satisfying, authentic sweetness. Those allergic to dairy can substitute vegan butter.

Bourbon Shortbread

- Nonstick cooking spray
- 1 cup, plus 2 Tbsp granulated sugar
- 1/2 cup brown sugar
- 3/4 cup butter (1 1/2 sticks), softened or melted
- 2 large eggs
- 1 Tbsp bourbon
- 1 1/2 cups all-purpose flour
- 1/2 tsp kosher salt
- 1/2 cup pecans, chopped and toasted

Total time: 45-50 minutes
Serves 12

Heat oven to 350 F.

Line a 10-inch cast-iron skillet with aluminum foil, fold down around edges/sides, spray foil with nonstick spray.

In a large mixing bowl, mix 1 cup granulated sugar and brown sugar, add melted butter. Using a hand mixer, beat mixture until it is fluffy, add eggs one at a time.

Add bourbon — you may use less if desired — and mix to ensure even distribution.

In a separate bowl, sift flour and salt. Add to the batter mixing thoroughly again with mixer.

Spread the dough, which will be tacky/sticky into your foil-lined skillet. An offset spatula sprayed with nonstick cooking spray is helpful.

Top the dough with chopped pecans and remaining 2 Tbsp of sugar.

Bake until slightly brown on top, about 35 minutes, depending on your oven.

Cool shortbread in the skillet on a cooling rack.

Once cool, using foil overhang, remove from skillet.

Remove the foil prior to slicing and serving.

Submitted by: Judy Willett, The Fresno Bee

Favorite thing about this recipe:
Tender and crumbly.

Marie's Biscotti

photo on page 111

- 1/2 cup butter-flavored shortening
- 4 Tbsp butter
- 1 cup sugar
- 3 eggs
- 1 tsp anise flavoring (or flavoring of your choice)
- 3 cup flour
- 3 tsp baking powder
- 1/2 tsp salt
- 1 cup chopped almonds (or nut of your choice)

Total time: 45 minutes
Yields 3 1/2-4 dozen cookies

Heat oven to 350 F.

Mix shortening, butter and sugar until creamy.

Add one egg at a time, mixing well after each.

Add flavoring, mix well.

Add 1 cup of flour at a time and 1 tsp of baking power, mixing well after each. Add salt, chopped nuts.

On floured board, roll dough into two rolls the length of your cookie sheet, press top down and bake for 30 minutes.

While still warm, slice diagonally and turn on their side.

Return to oven, bake 12 minutes.

Take out, turn over, bake again for 6 minutes. Cool.

Store in an airtight container or freeze.

Variations: Add 1 tsp cinnamon and 1 cup chopped dried cranberries.

Submitted by: Marie Cassano, The Fresno Bee

Favorite thing about this recipe: One-bowl method.

Double Chocolate Cream Pie

photo on page 110
- 1 premade Oreo pie crust

Filling
- 1/3 cup heavy cream
- 2 Tbsp cocoa
- 1 Tbsp vanilla extract
- 8 oz bittersweet chocolate, broken into chunks
- 1 1/2 cups heavy cream
- 1 Tbsp sugar
- 1/8 tsp salt

Topping
- 1 cup heavy cream
- 2 Tbsp powdered sugar
- Chocolate curls

Total time: 1 hour, 30 minutes
Serves 8

Make filling: In a medium bowl, microwave heavy cream for 30 seconds. Add cocoa and vanilla and stir. Set aside.

In separate bowl, microwave broken chocolate chunks 30 seconds. Stir chocolate. Microwave 30 more seconds or until chocolate has melted.

Stir the melted chocolate into the cocoa mixture and mix well.

Whip the heavy cream, sugar and salt until soft peaks form. Fold 1/2 of the heavy cream into the chocolate mixture. Beat remaining heavy cream for 10 seconds.

Fold whipped heavy cream into chocolate until no white streaks remain.

For the topping, whip heavy cream and sugar together until soft peaks form. Set aside.

Spread the chocolate filling evenly into the premade Oreo pie crust. Drop dollops of whipped cream on top. Top dollops with shaved chocolate curls. Refrigerate 1 hour before serving.

Submitted by: Vickie Maxwell, The Fresno Bee

Favorite thing about this recipe: It's very easy to make and meets my chocolate cravings.

Lavish Latte Lava Cake

photo on page 111

Cake

- 1 cup flour
- 1/4 cup cocoa
- 2 tsp baking powder
- 3/4 cup coconut sugar
- 1/4 tsp salt
- 1/2 cup almond milk
- 4 Tbsp butter, melted
- 2 tsp vanilla
- 1/4 cup dark chocolate chips
- 1/4 cup white chocolate chips

Latte Sauce

- 1/4 cup cocoa powder
- 2/4 cup coconut sugar
- 1 tsp vanilla
- 1 3/4 cup coffee, boiling

Total time: 1 hour, 20 minutes
Serves 8

Lightly grease 3- or 4-quart slow cooker.

In medium-size bowl, mix flour, cocoa, baking powder, coconut sugar and salt. Stir in almond milk, melted butter and vanilla. When just combined, place in slow cooker.

Mix dark and white chocolate chips and press into the top of batter.

Make latte sauce: Combine cocoa powder, coconut sugar, vanilla and coffee. Pour over the top of mixture and place lid on slow cooker. Cook on low.

Begin checking at 1 hour. Depending on size of slow cooker, time will vary from 1-2 hours.

Remove with large spoon and arrange sauce over top. Serve with vanilla ice cream if desired.

Submitted by: Stacy Renee Lucas, The Fresno Bee

Favorite thing about this recipe: It really is lavish. No one guesses that it was so easy to make something that tastes like a molten lava cake from the finest restaurant.

White Almond Wedding Cake

- 15.25-oz box Betty Crocker Super Moist French Vanilla Cake Mix
- 1 cup all-purpose flour
- 1 cup sugar
- 3/4 tsp salt
- 1 tsp baking soda
- 1 1/3 cup vanilla almond milk
- 5.3 oz vanilla almond milk yogurt
- 4 Tbsp butter, melted
- 1 tsp almond extract
- 1 tsp vanilla extract
- 5 egg whites

Total time: 1 hour
Serves 12

Heat oven to 325 F.

Grease and flour cake pans.

In large bowl, stir together the cake mix, flour, sugar, salt and baking soda. Add in milk, yogurt, butter, almond and vanilla extract and egg whites.

Beat with electric mixer on low until moistened.

Pour in cake pans. Bake 45 minutes, until toothpick comes out clean.

Submitted by: Cassie Fuller, Fort Worth Star-Telegram

Favorite thing about this recipe: It's easy.

Boy Scout Cobbler

photo on page 106

- Canned fruit of your choice (apple, peach, raspberry, blackberry)
- Cake mix (yellow or spice)
- 12-oz can soda
- 4 Tbsp butter, sliced thin

Total time: 1 hour
Serves 10

Prepare campfire or heat oven to 350 F.

In a Dutch oven (over fire) or casserole dish (in oven), pour the fruit (or fruits) of your choice.

Pour the cake mix on top of fruit and then pour the soda on top. Slightly mix so the cake mix is distributed into the fruit and soda.

Add butter on top.

If using a campfire, place Dutch oven on 14 coals and place 10 coals on the lid.

If using an oven, cook uncovered for approximately 45 minutes, checking after 30 minutes.

Check consistency by sticking the middle and verifying stick comes out clean.

Let set 15 minutes and serve warm with vanilla ice cream if desired.

Note on Flavors

Spice cake mix and Sprite go well. Yellow mix and Dr Pepper or Cherry Coke go well. Try combinations as you see fit, I have not found a bad one yet.

Submitted by: Gary Goldstein, Fort Worth Star-Telegram

Favorite thing about this recipe: Easy camping recipe. Great for youth to cook.

Mom's Christmas Cookies

Cookies

- 1 cup shortening or butter
- 1 cup sugar
- 1 large egg
- 2 Tbsp milk
- 1 Tbsp vanilla extract
- 3 cups all-purpose flour
- 1 1/2 tsp baking powder
- 1/2 tsp salt

Frosting

- 2 cups powdered sugar
- 1/2 tsp vanilla
- 2 Tbsp milk

Total time: 1 hour
Yields 24 cookies

In large bowl, beat shortening or butter and sugar with mixer on medium speed until smooth and creamy. Beat in egg, milk and vanilla until well blended.

In medium bowl, combine flour, baking powder and salt. Gradually add to shortening mixture on low speed until blended.

Divide dough into three pieces. Wrap in plastic wrap. Chill 1 hour.

Heat oven to 375 F.

Roll 1 piece of dough at a time on lightly floured surface to 1/8-inch thickness. Cut dough with 2- to 3-inch floured cookie cutters. Place 1 inch apart on ungreased baking sheets.

Bake 5 to 9 minutes or until edges begin to brown. Cool 2 minutes. Remove to wire rack to cool completely. Decorate as desired.

Submitted by: Krista Reed, Fort Worth Star-Telegram

Favorite thing about this recipe: Mom used to make them all the time for Christmas when I was a kid. Now that she has passed, I make them for my kids.

Cranberry Jell-O Salad

photo on page 105

- 3-oz box lemon Jell-O
- 3-oz box cherry Jell-O
- 2 cups boiling water
- 1 large can crushed pineapple, drained (reserve 1/2 juice)
- 2 cups sugar
- 1 lb fresh cranberries
- 1/2 cup celery, chopped
- 1 large red apple, chopped
- 1 cup pecans, chopped

Total time: 30 minutes
Serves 16

Combine Jell-O with boiling water; then add pineapple and sugar and reserved pineapple juice, stir well.

In food processor, grind up cranberries and add to mixture. Add chopped celery, apple and nuts. Chill (overnight, if possible) until congealed.

Submitted by: Kelley Cates, Fort Worth Star-Telegram

Favorite thing about this recipe: Family favorite.

Jell-O Dream Cake

- 1 box French vanilla cake mix
- 1 1/2 cups boiling water
- 1 small box strawberry Jell-O
- 10 oz strawberry pop
- 2 cups milk, cold
- 1 large vanilla instant pudding
- 1/2 tsp vanilla extract
- 12 oz Cool Whip
- Fresh strawberries

Total time: 1 hour
Serves 12-14

Make cake per directions on box until almost done. Boil water, add strawberry Jell-O and mix well, add strawberry pop.

Poke cake with fork or wooden spoon. Pour mixture over cake. Chill 20 minutes.

Make topping: Mix milk with pudding and add vanilla. Fold in Cool Whip. Spread over cake.

Top with fresh berries and chill 6 hours.

Submitted by: Kelley Cates, Fort Worth Star-Telegram

Favorite thing about this recipe: Tastes like summer.

Coconut Cream Pie with Chocolate Drizzle

photo on page 109

- 1 pie crust, baked

Toasted Coconut Topping

- 1/2 cup flaked sweetened coconut

Coconut Cream

- 2 cups coconut milk
- 1 1/2 cups half-and-half
- 5 egg yolks
- 3/4 cup sugar
- 4 Tbsp cornstarch
- 1 Tbsp butter
- 1 1/2 cups flaked sweetened coconut
- 1 1/2 tsp vanilla
- 1/4 tsp salt
- Hershey's chocolate syrup

Total time: 2 hours
Serves 8-10

Prepare pie crust according to blind-baking instructions of recipe.

Make toasted coconut topping: Heat oven to 350 F. Spread coconut evenly on a rimmed baking sheet. Place into oven for 8-10 minutes until coconut just begins to turn brown. Set aside to cool.

Make coconut custard: Pour coconut milk and half-and-half into a liquid measuring cup. Add egg yolks and whisk together with milks. Set aside.

In a heavy-bottom saucepan, add sugar and cornstarch. Stir egg and milk mixture together once more and then over medium-low heat, slowly add to the sugar and cornstarch, whisking together constantly until thick.

Bring mixture to a boil. Switch to a rubber spatula and continue to stir constantly. Boil about 1 minute.

Remove from heat, and add butter, coconut, vanilla and salt. Stir until well mixed.

Spread custard into pie crust. Cover with plastic wrap and chill in the refrigerator until set, at least 45 minutes.

Refrigerate until ready to serve.

When ready to serve, top with toasted coconut and drizzle with Hershey's syrup.

Submitted by: Kathleen Greene, Fort Worth Star-Telegram

Favorite thing about this recipe: Burst of flavor!

Cheese Flan

photo on page 106

- 3/4 cup sugar
- 1/4 cup water
- 5 large eggs
- 8 oz cream cheese
- 14-oz can sweetened condensed milk
- 5-oz can evaporated milk
- 2 tsp vanilla
- Berries and whipped cream for garnishing

Total time: 13 hours, 30 minutes
Serves 8

Heat oven to 350 F.

In a heavy-bottom pan, combine sugar and water and cook at medium heat until sugar caramelizes to a medium brown color. Be careful; the sugar will be very hot!

While the sugar is still hot, pour it into a 9x5x3 inch loaf pan; tip the pan so that the caramel goes about 1 inch up the sides, but leaving most of it in the bottom. Set aside to cool.

In a blender, blend eggs, cream cheese, condensed milk, evaporated milk and vanilla until smooth. Pour the egg mixture over the cooled caramel in the pan. Place the loaf pan into a larger pan and create a water bath adding about 1 1/2 inches of water to the larger pan.

Bake for 60-70 minutes or until custard is firm. If it is getting too brown on top, loosely cover the flan pan (not the water bath) with foil. When cooked, remove loaf pan from the larger pan and allow it to cool at room temperature for at least an hour.

Wrap pan in plastic wrap and refrigerate for at least 12 hours.

When completely cooled, run a very thin knife around the outside of the flan, cover the loaf pan with a serving plate and invert flan onto the plate. Gently tap the bottom and sides of the pan to release the flan. Using a rubber spatula, scrape all the delicious sauce that remains in the bottom of the pan onto the flan.

Garnish with whipped cream and fresh berries.

Submitted by: Bob Rosar, Fort Worth Star-Telegram

Favorite thing about this recipe: I grew up in Miami where flan is at every restaurant and home. This cheese flan is served at "special" occasions because it is extra rich and creamy. It reminds me of my many Latin friends in South Florida.

Lemon and Toffee Chip Ice Cream

photo on page 109

- 2 cups heavy whipping cream
- 14-oz can condensed milk
- 12-oz can evaporated milk
- 1/3 cup almonds, ground
- 1/2 cup lemon cheesecake liqueur
- 1 Tbsp grated lemon rind
- Juice of 1 lemon
- 1/2 tsp lemon extract
- 1/2 cup broken toffee chips

Total time: 6 hours
Serves 6

In a large bowl, beat whipping cream until stiff peaks form. Pour in condensed milk and evaporated milk, stir until combined. Add ground almonds, lemon cheesecake liqueur, lemon rind, lemon juice and lemon extract and stir until well mixed.

Pour into a container and freeze for approximately 6 hours or overnight.

Serve with a sprinkling of toffee chips and a drizzle of lemon cheesecake liqueur if desired.

Submitted by: Fiona Green, Fort Worth Star-Telegram

Favorite thing about this recipe: Ice cream is my favorite dessert at any time of year. It is light and creamy and satisfies my sweet tooth perfectly. This recipe is so easy a child could make it (perhaps without the liqueur) and it tastes amazing!

Amy's Scrumptious Apple Pie

- 2 discs pie dough, homemade pie dough or premade crusts
- 8 Gala apples, peeled, sliced in medium pieces
- 1 cup sugar
- 2 Tbsp fresh lemon juice
- 1/2 tsp ground cinnamon
- Dash of ground nutmeg
- 3 Tbsp flour
- 1-2 Tbsp butter, cubed
- 1 Tbsp cream (for top crust)
- 2 Tbsp sugar (for top crust)

Total time: 2 hours
Serves 8

Prepare pie dough if making from scratch. Divide and chill dough while preparing filling.

Heat oven to 425 F.

Into a large bowl, place peeled and sliced apples. Add sugar and lemon juice gradually to apples.

Allow about 5 minutes for juice from apples to surface. Add cinnamon, nutmeg. Stir gently. Mix in flour lightly.

Roll out the first pie crust. Place bottom crust in 9-inch pie tin.

Pour apple filling over bottom crust.

Dot filling with cubed butter.

Roll out top pie crust. Cut center with fancy pie cutter or small round biscuit cutter.

Place top pie crust over pie filling. Seal edges on both crusts by fluting.

Brush top of crust with cream. Sprinkle with sugar.

Cover pie crusts with a shield to prevent over-browning.

Place pie on a parchment covered sheet pan. Bake in preheated oven for 15 minutes. Reduce heat to 350 F and continue baking for about 45 minutes or until apples are bubbly and crust is nicely browned.

Remove from oven. Serve warm with a scoop of vanilla ice cream. Yummy!

Submitted by: Amy Vanderpoel, Fort Worth Star-Telegram

Favorite thing about this recipe: This homey apple pie is a favorite at our special family gatherings, especially at Thanksgiving. Everyone from little ones to adults like this pie. As our family grows, I now bake 2 apple pies!

Best Ever Pecan Pie

- 1 frozen pie crust
- 1/4 cup Karo dark syrup
- 1/4 cup Karo light syrup
- 1 1/4 cups sugar
- Pinch of salt
- 4 Tbsp unsalted butter, room temperature
- 3 eggs, room temperature
- 1 tsp vanilla
- 1 1/4 cups pecan halves

Total time: 1 hour, 15 minutes
Serves 8

Preheat oven 350 F.

Let pie crust come to room temperature.

Over medium heat, stir the syrups, sugar, salt and butter to a gentle boil.

In a large bowl, beat eggs.

Slowly pour the hot syrup mixture into the eggs and continue to stir.

Add vanilla.

Add pecans and stir.

Pour the ingredients into the pie crust. Bake for 45 minutes. Let cool.

Serve with vanilla ice cream, yum!

Submitted by: Paula Brown, The Island Packet

Favorite thing about this recipe: Quick and easy to make for last-minute.

Sundae Pie

- 12-oz can evaporated milk
- 12 oz semisweet chocolate chips
- 2 cups miniature marshmallows
- 1/2 tsp salt
- 1 box vanilla wafers
- 64 oz vanilla ice cream
- 1/2 cup nuts, chopped (optional)

Total time: 35 minutes
Serves 16-20

In a heavy pan, stir the milk, chocolate chips, marshmallows and salt over medium heat and let thicken. Cool to room temperature.

In a 9x13 pan, put down a layer of vanilla wafers, then 1/2 of the ice cream and 1/2 of the chocolate sauce. Repeat layer. Top with chopped nuts if desired and freeze.

Can use any flavor ice cream you would like.

Submitted by: Carol McBride, The Island Packet

Favorite thing about this recipe: It's creamy, gooey and crunchy!

Marvelous Macaroons

photo on page 105

- 1/2 cup butter, softened
- 4 oz cream cheese, softened
- 3/4 cup sugar
- 1 egg yolk
- 2 tsp fresh orange juice
- 2 tsp pure almond extract
- 1 1/4 cups flour
- 2 tsp baking powder
- 1/4 tsp salt
- 6 cups sweetened flaked coconut, divided

Total time: 2 hours, 30 minutes
Yields 30 macaroons

Beat butter, cream cheese and sugar at medium speed with electric mixer until blended.

Add egg yolk, orange juice, almond extract and beat until blended.

Combine flour, baking powder and salt and add to butter batter; beat until blended.

Stir in 3 cups of coconut then cover and chill batter for 2 hours in refrigerator.

Heat oven to 350 F.

Finely chop remaining 3 cups of coconut.

Shape batter into 2-inch balls and roll in remaining chopped coconut.

Bake on ungreased baking sheets for 11-13 minutes or until the macaroons are lightly browned. Cool 2 minutes then move to wire racks.

Once thoroughly cool, place in cookie tin.

Submitted by: Barre Wright, The Island Packet

Favorite thing about this recipe: Very tasty and easy to make.